NSPCC

Policy Practice Research Series

Child Protection and Education

By Mary Baginsky
Foreword by Professor Olive Stevenson

The author

Mary Baginsky is a Senior Research Officer in NSPCC's Research Group. After a brief teaching career she has conducted a variety of research and evaluation projects mainly within an educational context, but also those with a legal, criminological and social welfare focus. Her current research interests are the role of the school in a multi-agency approach to child protection and the support of adolescents who have been subjected to abuse.

The NSPCC is the UK's leading charity specialising in child protection and the prevention of cruelty to children.

The NSPCC exists to prevent children from suffering abuse and is working for a future for children free from cruelty.

First published 2000 by the NSPCC
42 Curtain Road
London
EC2A 3NH

Tel: 020 7825 2500
Fax: 020 7825 2525
Email: cprt@nspcc.org.uk

Registered charity number 216401

Director and Chief Executive: Mary Marsh

Design by Red Stone

ISBN 1-84228-008-2

NSPCC

Cruelty to children must stop. FULL STOP.

Foreword

This is an important publication which should be read widely by teachers and those, such as members of Area Child Protection Committees, who are concerned with the protection of children from abuse. It is important because it describes and analyses some critical issues which have to be grasped if schools are to be effective in safeguarding vulnerable children. Ensuring that systems and structures are working well in this respect is complex, the more so because constant organisational change has been a feature of the past decades and of the present time. Nowhere is this more evident than in the educational system and its relations with other agencies concerned with child welfare. In my view, this is currently the most pressing matter in the challenge of *Working Together* for children's protection.

As this survey shows, there are two important strands in the present difficulties. First, the structural changes by which schools acquired greater independence from local education authorities have raised a series of urgent questions concerning, for example, the allocation of funds by schools for child protection (such as teachers' attendance at case conferences) and the responsibility and accountability of school governors. Secondly, there seems at present to be an inherent tension between the drive to improve standards (and results) in the general population of children and the special needs of children who are, in a sense, 'a drag' on the rest. Yet amongst such children are a significant proportion who are suffering at home and for whom the vigilance and concern of teachers is a key element in their protection. There must be a way to acknowledge and reward mainstream schools who contribute to such children's well-being.

These are but two of the issues which this publication highlights.

In Chapter 5, there is a valuable account of the implications of the Children Act, 1989, for child welfare. The Act reaffirms and consolidates a key concept, now firmly entrenched in official policy, that good practice in child welfare necessitates effective communication and co-ordination between professionals and agencies. It is self-evident that teachers cannot 'go it alone' in child protection. This means that all the parties have a responsibility to work together. Indeed, when inquires into the deaths of children are set up, the effectiveness with which agencies work together can be one of the grounds for criticism. It is apparent that much needs to be done to improve, in particular, relations between schools and Social Services Departments. This needs better understanding of each others' roles and constraints so that sensible arrangements for co-operation can be agreed.

I have much hope that this thoughtful report will give focus to a constructive debate on an urgent matter.

Olive Stevenson
Professor Emeritus of Social Work Studies, University of Nottingham

Acknowledgements

The author is indebted to the many people who contributed to this study. This report contains the results of three surveys which could not have been carried out without the support of many people and it would be impossible to acknowledge all of them.

In the early stages of this work I consulted widely and I am particularly grateful for the comments and perspectives given by Chris Eissen of Mount Carmel School in Islington and Marysia Eminowicz of Brent Local Education Authority, and on an international level by Shoshana Zimmerman of the Ministry of Education, Jerusalem. I then returned to NSPCC Library to follow up what I had learned and the staff there made this task so much easier.

I worked very closely with Keith Hodgkinson, who was jointly responsible for the work on initial teacher training and valued the fact that he could so generously share his wisdom and insights.

The fact that we dealt with three surveys in a reasonably short time owes much to the efforts of Suzanne Kayne and I shall always be very grateful for all the support, advice and humour which she shared with me while she was a secretary with NSPCC's Research Group. Since then Caroline Boyle has had the responsibility of seeing this through to completion and has done so with remarkable efficiency and patience.

Over the past months various people have been asked to look at the report and I appreciate the effort which they all put into this task. Throughout the project David Ring of Hertfordshire LEA allowed me to consult with him and he then gave me the benefit of his comments on an earlier draft. Ann Sinclair-Taylor of the Department of Education at the University of Warwick, Professor Tricia David of Canterbury Christ Church University College and Dr Pat Cawson Head of the Research Group at NSPCC volunteered to plough through the draft and comment on it. All of this they did meticulously and went beyond this to give me their support.

However, unless hundreds of people had thought the work was sufficiently important to bother to complete yet another questionnaire which fell onto their desks I would have nothing on which to base this report. I cannot name them but I am extremely grateful that they were prepared to help in this way, as were the SCITTs managers, who agreed to be interviewed so that Keith Hodgkinson and myself could explore their initial responses in more detail, and the two groups of students who shared their experiences with me.

I also want to acknowledge the support which I always get from my family, but this time it was particularly significant. William was able to share insights gained from his role as a designated teacher, sometimes bringing the practical constraints up against my ideas of ideal practice, and he then went on to give me the benefit of his excellent editorial skills.

Even with all this support, if there are flaws in this report they are my own.

Contents

Tables

Summary of research and findings

Over the past two decades schools have increasingly been drawn into working with other agencies on child protection issues, but there is an obvious need for research which will examine the realities of schools' involvement in the child protection process. NSPCC plans to conduct a research project which will examine the ways in which schools and Social Services Departments work together over child protection matters. It will allow many of the strands which have been examined individually to be studied in a co-ordinated way and provide practitioners, policy makers and researchers with a clearer understanding of the role of the education service (after a period of considerable change) in relation to child protection than is available at the present time. As a prelude to this it was important to identify how schools and LEAs were approaching the area of child protection and to begin to examine the training which teachers receive to prepare and support them in this work.

The evolving role of education in relation to child protection

This chapter examines:

■ the ways in which schools have been given greater responsibility in relation to child protection

■ earlier research which has been conducted on this subject

■ the impact of educational reforms on the ability of schools to meet their responsibilities

■ the need for further research.

Child protection training in initial teacher training: results of a preliminary survey

In 1996 specific coverage of child protection issues was discussed as a future requirement on initial teacher training (ITT) courses. Subsequently, Circular 4/98 *Teaching: High Status, High Standards* (Department for Education and Employment, 1998) laid down the Secretary of State for Education and Employment's requirements for all ITT courses. There is one standard in the new ITT curriculum which relates directly to child protection and this states that:

...for all courses, those to be awarded Qualified Teacher Status should, when assessed, demonstrate that they have a working knowledge and understanding of teachers' legal liabilities and responsibilities.

Despite the requirement of Circular 4/98 it is widely believed that those standards that deal with issues of child welfare are not accorded equal status with their academic equivalents. But teachers' responsibilities for child protection have increased and, as the survey of teachers' attitudes showed, there is some concern about the training which occurs on teacher training courses. In an attempt to reach a better understanding of the child protection input on these courses a survey was undertaken.

Early in the autumn term 1997 a questionnaire and explanatory letter were sent to all higher education institutions providing ITT according to the Universities Council for the Education of Teachers (UCET). The UCET list did not specify individual courses and so multiple copies were sent to each institutional contact named by UCET, although the intention was that they would be passed to the most appropriate person to try to ensure coverage of all relevant courses within each institution. In the event 128 replies were received from 68 institutions (82% of institutions providing ITT courses at that time). The same questionnaire was sent to the newer school-based training courses, School Centred Initial Teacher Training courses (SCITTs). SCITTs were introduced in 1993 as an alternative route to achieving Qualified Teacher Status. Based on consortia of schools the intention is to provide the opportunity to design, organise and provide school-based courses for graduates. At the time when the survey was sent out 26 consortia were providing such courses, covering both primary and secondary sectors. The questionnaire was addressed to the managers in these consortia. Fourteen of the 26 replied, representing a 54% response rate.

On the courses based in institutions of higher education:

■ The overwhelming majority (118, 92%) of responding higher education courses claimed to have an element dedicated to child protection issues, with 115 of these courses reporting that it was a compulsory part. However, this means that ten courses, of which seven were PGCE courses, had no coverage.

■ Most courses (66%) covered it after the first assessed school placement, with the rest almost equally spread between courses doing so before this placement and those covering it after the final placement.

■ Most courses offered more than one hour, but it was just one hour or less on 17% of courses. One course offered an eight-hour element, but this was part of a more general conference on child protection and related issues. Perhaps surprisingly there was no significant difference between the length of the input on PGCE courses and that on the longer degree courses.

■ Over 80% of these courses were taught by, or had some input from, an outside speaker. Most of these were social workers, but head teachers and other senior teachers were frequent presenters. Other professionals involved in this work included specialists from Local Education Authorities, the Police, NSPCC, and the Probation Service. Very few courses were currently using their own staff to teach this subject but there was certainly some concern amongst respondents about how they would be able to continue to meet the costs of outside speakers and comments which indicated that they may have to consider providing it themselves.

■ Those responding to the questionnaire were asked to assess the possible long term effects on their courses in the light of the requirements of Circular 4/98 (and their Welsh equivalents). Well over half of the courses did not think that the new provisions would make any difference to what was taught in relation to child protection, with 31% estimating that there would be an overall increase.

The responses from SCITTs were similar in some respects but:

■ Only ten of the fourteen respondents claimed to have a child protection element.

■ Most of the courses covered the subject very early on in the autumn term.

■ The time devoted to the subject varied considerably. Four courses spent three to four hours on child protection, one spent one to two hours, two spent two hours and three reported spending less than one hour on the subject.

■ The teaching styles adopted were similar to those in higher education institutions. Six schemes used a school teacher or head teacher and four used a specialist, although in the questionnaire there were no details provided about the specialisms that they held.

The responses from SCITTs had indicated some degree of uncertainty on the part of those running these courses about what they should be covering on child protection issues. Because of this and the relatively low response rate from SCITTs it was decided to interview the responding SCITT managers to explore the areas in more detail. The interviews indicated that, with the exception of one primary course and one secondary course, training in relation to child protection was extremely patchy. In addition they seemed to place considerable responsibility with the schools for preparing students, although no SCITTs used designated teachers from their consortia for this input.

Schools' response to child protection

A questionnaire was sent to 385 schools to follow up their attitudes to child protection issues, some of which had been identified in earlier research. Eighty-five per cent of schools replied. The main findings were:

■ All but one of the 327 responding schools had a designated teacher with responsibility for child protection. The one exception was a state primary school. In 50% of schools this was the head teacher, although there was a significant difference between primary and secondary schools. In 93% of primary schools the head teacher was also the designated teacher, while in the secondary sector the figure was 10%. Secondary schools were far more likely to have appointed a deputy head teacher into the designated role (65% compared with 4% in primary schools).

■ The overwhelming majority of schools (94%) have a child protection policy in place and 99% have established procedures, in accordance with their policies and/or those of their LEAs.

■ Of the 263 schools that had received an OFSTED inspection at the time of the research, 63% were sure that the policy had been inspected by their OFSTED teams; 11% were sure that it had not been, 16% did not know and in 10% of schools no policy had been in place at the time of the inspection.

■ Of the 327 schools in the study, 93% (305) said they would usually be represented at case conferences, but a number of practical concerns were raised by many schools.

■ While the respondents were reasonably confident that they would be able to recognise signs of abuse in children in their care and act on them, most (88%) had some concerns that this would not be the case for all teachers.

■ Eighty-seven per cent of schools in the study had some concern about teachers' own vulnerability when they report abuse, with more than half of these indicating a reasonably high level of concern.

■ Just under two-thirds of schools reported some degree of uncertainty about when to contact Social Services in relation to a child protection concern, and for half of these it was quite a major problem. Eighty-four per cent of schools expressed some level of concern about the way the different agencies involved in the child protection process communicated with each other, with two-thirds of these being very concerned.

■ Schools were asked to say if they had any concerns about the possibility of teachers trying to handle child protection issues on their own without reference to the procedures in place or the appropriate colleague. Although over half of respondents (55%) thought that it could happen, most did not regard it as a major concern and believed that once teachers identified a concern they would pass it on to the designated teacher.

■ Eighty-eight per cent of schools reported having some concerns about how they could best support children when they disclose abuse to staff, with well over half saying that it was something which caused considerable concern. Overall, 90% of the schools were concerned about how best to support children subsequent to disclosing abuse. Again, for over half, it was something which was causing a fairly high level of disquiet and, in an ideal situation, the majority would like to work closely with Social Services and their LEAs to reach a solution.

■ The majority of schools (82%) were concerned about how best to support teachers who are faced with dealing with children who may have experienced abuse, with half viewing it as a major issue. Most schools thought they needed additional counselling or advice either from within the school or their LEAs, although many also thought that Social Services could be involved.

■ Most schools (79%) said they were concerned about how to handle accusations made by pupils against teachers; the majority indicated that these concerns were not only of a reasonably high level, but that they had increased in recent years as some high profile cases had attracted media attention.

■ Ninety-two per cent of schools said they had some concerns about how to maintain relationships with parents when the schools were involved in child protection cases and two-thirds of respondents were very concerned about this.

■ Just over 70% of schools were concerned about the pressures on their time which inhibited their ability to get to know pupils and for half of these it was proving to be an increasing problem.

■ Three-quarters of responding schools were also concerned about the time taken dealing with child protection issues and for most of them there were particular concerns about the pressures on certain members of staff.

■ The overwhelming majority of designated teachers with responsibility for child protection (92%) had received appropriate training. Most designated teachers had been on more than one course and were generally positive about them, especially when higher level training had enabled them to train side-by-side with other professionals involved in the child protection process.

■ Two-thirds of schools replied that other members of staff had received training, most of which had been school-based, although there were examples of whole staff training by LEAs and multi-agency led training of school staff.

■ Just over a fifth of schools (22%) said one or more members of their governing bodies had received training, most of which had been provided by LEAs specifically for governors, although there were examples of other models of training provided by Social Services, the Education Welfare Service and others.

■ Schools wanted all teachers to receive regular training in recognising the signs of abuse in children as well as in how to respond to suspicions and disclosures. Alongside this were calls for particular attention to be paid to students on teaching practice placements and newly qualified teachers within structured induction programmes.

■ Ninety per cent of respondents claimed to have at least one person with whom they could discuss a possible referral. Nine per cent had no one and they would all have welcomed such a person, and the remaining one per cent claimed not to need such support. The most frequently mentioned source of support was a social worker from the local Social Services team (43%); 25% mentioned an education welfare officer; 23% mentioned other colleagues; 18% referred to a member of the LEA staff and 6% identified the school nurse. Other individuals and agencies mentioned and included other health professionals and members of governing bodies, particularly those with relevant professional expertise.

■ Sixty-five per cent of responding schools would welcome more help and information on child protection issues, especially from Local Education Authorities, Social Services Departments, Area Child Protection Committees and NSPCC.

The role of LEAs in child protection

A questionnaire was sent to all LEAs, including Unitary Authorities which were due to come into existence in April 1998, and replies were received from 85% of LEAs/Unitary Authorities which were canvassed. The results of this survey are summarised below:

■ The majority of authorities (98% of respondents) replied that they did provide written guidance of some sort to schools, although only 56% of authorities claimed to have drawn up a specific document for education, with most of the others distributing ACPC procedures to schools and a few sending schools information circulars which had been prepared for training courses.

■ All the authorities were represented on their ACPCs and the guidance prepared for schools all followed the principles of ACPC guidelines.

■ The responses clearly indicated that LEAs took differing approaches to their relationships with both the then grant maintained schools and independent schools. For example, 15% of LEAs said they had offered training and consultation to independent schools on behalf of their ACPCs, but it had been declined. In most cases non-LEA schools would pay for such training, but there were LEAs continuing to provide the same child protection services to grant maintained schools as they had before the change in status – and without any charge. A small number of respondents actually expressed uncertainty about their responsibility for these schools, particularly independent schools, and there were certainly LEAs very reluctant to accept any responsibility for grant maintained schools.

■ All LEAs said they offered a consultation service to the schools in their areas and, as indicated above, this would often be available to grant maintained schools and in some cases to independent schools. Eighty-seven per cent of LEAs said they included details about the service in relevant documentation sent to schools. In 80% of LEAs this was provided by the Education Social Work/Welfare Services, although in some cases this was in conjunction with other agencies such as the Education Psychology Service or a specific child protection service or other LEA staff. In the other LEAs this service was provided entirely by others such as child protection co-ordinators, Children's Services managers and workers in School Support sections.

■ Ninety per cent of LEAs included training on child protection issues as a standard item in their training programme, although a third of authorities made it clear that this was solely or largely provided by Social Services or on a multi-agency basis and many other authorities employed independent trainers who sometimes worked alongside Education or Social Services staff. In addition there were many comments indicating that LEAs would not be able to continue with the current level of training now that GEST (Grants for Education Support and Training) funding had ceased.

■ Ninety-five per cent provided training for designated teachers; 70% provided training for pastoral staff; 65% provided training for all teaching staff, 64% provided training for all school staff, usually where requested; 58% provided training for peripatetic staff and 45% of LEAs extended this training to youth workers, home tutors and others having direct contact with children. In addition, 66% of LEAs provided training for school governors, some being in response to governors' requests for clarification of their responsibilities in relation to any allegations of misconduct by head teachers, while others said the emphasis was on policies and procedures.

■ LEAs were asked to provide details of the proportion of schools located in their areas that had been represented on child protection training during the past three years. Seventy-eight per cent of LEAs were able to provide this information in relation to their own schools. In 22% of these authorities they had all been represented and in a further 9% 90% or more of their schools had been represented. However, in 13% of LEAs 50% or fewer primary schools had had a member of staff at any appropriate training. As far as LEA secondary and special schools were concerned the proportions of all schools represented were somewhat higher. In 32% of LEAs all secondary schools had been represented and 45% of special schools. Of concern, however, was the fact that in 19% of LEAs 50% of secondary schools had not attended and in 13% of LEAs this was the case in relation to special schools. Overall 10% of LEAs had had fewer than 25% of their schools represented on training in the past three years.

■ Over 90% of authorities have a procedure in place which requires designated teachers to make referrals directly to Social Services, although in most cases they are then required to notify the responsible officer in the LEA. Other patterns which emerged from the survey were authorities which required schools to make any referral via the Education Social Work Service/Education Welfare Service or to contact the responsible officer in the LEA who then had contact with Social Services. Only one LEA set out all three routes as alternatives with schools choosing the one they wished to use.

Seeing beyond the circulars

Although the role of the school in relation to child protection has been set out in guidance issued by the Government, the reality of day-to-day practice depends on a number of factors. These include the training which teachers have received and the confidence they feel about operating in this area; the relationships which are established with Social Services and the perceptions which each agency has of the other; the priority which schools and LEAs give to this aspect of their work; and shared understanding between schools and Social Services about what constitutes an appropriate referral. Both services have experienced a period of considerable change over the past decade and this has had implications for multi-agency work. Although difficulties are identified it is also recognised that there are opportunities to improve the existing situations. It is vital that a planned approach to training teachers in child protection is adopted, which would extend beyond initial teacher training courses to LEAs and influence their provision for newly qualified teachers as well as their in-service provision for all teachers. The other priority is to maintain a high level of training for designated teachers who should be the source of experience, knowledge and support in relation to child protection in schools.

The research has shown that schools are willing partners in child protection but they want support for their students and for themselves. This could be provided in a number of ways, and governments in this country and elsewhere have introduced initiatives aimed at providing support more effectively. It is hoped that these will also contribute to an improved level of multi-agency practice and, in the long term, a truly integrated approach to the welfare of children.

Recommendations

The concluding chapter contains a series of recommendations arising from the findings of the research studies in the three arenas, which should be adopted immediately:

■ OFSTED has a responsibility to inspect child protection policies and procedures in schools and LEAs to judge whether they conform to the guidance given by the DfEE. It is important that all teams have a consistent approach to the task and that they include discussions with representatives of the school community to ensure that they have a full understanding of the policies, procedures and their implementation.

■ Teachers have a vital place at case conferences and it is important for LEAs to support their presence in every way possible, including a funding formula which recognises that some schools need to attend a significant number of child protection conferences and associated meetings.

■ There is a clear need for schools and Social Services Departments to liaise over the timing of conferences and the information required from each.

■ All schools should receive guidance on their responsibilities to make sure that newly qualified teachers, newly appointed members of staff and students on placements with them are aware of their child protection policies and procedures.

■ Training for all teachers and other members of school communities in child protection should be an ongoing activity. Particular emphasis should be on the identification of the signs and symptoms of abuse as well as on how to deal with putting together various elements that may have aroused their suspicions.

■ All teachers should receive some training about case conferences and their role in these and associated meetings.

■ Support should be provided for teachers in:
    dealing with parents on matters of child protection
    supporting children and young people who report abuse
    supporting colleagues who deal with child protection issues.

■ There needs to be improved liaison between Social Services Departments and schools in the hope of improving each service's understanding of the other, combined with a more extensive use of multi-agency training for all teachers and social workers.

■ When Social Services Departments receive a referral, they should inform the school about the action taken or if no action is taken the reasons.

■ A regular reminder should be sent from LEAs to schools about schools' responsibilities in relation to child protection issues and the training opportunities that are available.

■ A helpline, or other form of support service, should be introduced in every area to give schools the opportunity to discuss concerns before they decide if it is appropriate to make a referral.

■ Further work is needed to identify the support that independent schools receive in dealing with child protection issues and the additional support that may be required.

■ Student teachers and newly qualified members of the profession should receive appropriate training to help them deal with any demands they will encounter in their early years in the classroom. This needs to be supported by high quality materials designed to ensure that all teachers have a solid understanding of the issues involved and which could subsequently be used as reference material.

1 The evolving role of education in relation to child protection

Background

Under the Children Act 1989 local authorities have a general duty to safeguard and promote the welfare of children within their area who are in need and, so far as is consistent with their duty, to promote the upbringing of such children by their families. Local Authority Social Services Departments (SSDs) are subject to specific statutory duties in relation to children, namely to investigate reports of children suffering, or likely to suffer, significant harm and to take appropriate action to safeguard or promote the child's welfare. They have a duty to provide services and prevent children in their area suffering ill-treatment or neglect and to reduce the need to bring court proceedings in respect of them.

However, a number of other agencies are involved in child protection work and over the years there has been a deliberate attempt to co-ordinate action and to encourage and develop inter-agency work and make it more effective. One of the key agencies is the school. Apart from their homes, children spend more time in school than in any other environment. The behavioural and physical indicators that suggest mistreatment of a child are likely to be evident within the school setting. The importance of this has long been recognised in many quarters. The Chairman's report on the Lucy Gates inquiry (London Borough of Bexley and Greenwich and Bexley Health Authority, 1982) commented on the need for schools to be able to recognise child abuse. The Richard Fraser inquiry (London Borough of Lambeth et al, 1982) referred to the lack of a real understanding by school staff on the procedures which should be followed in the case of suspected injuries and the Beckford Report (London Borough of Brent and Brent Health Authority, 1985) drew attention to the interaction between a child's private life and its response to school and went on to comment that the '... fear of crossing the vague boundaries which divide the social worker from school inhibits each side from a collaboration which is necessary to them both'. Soon after that report Peter Maher (1987) wrote that 'it is an unfortunate fact that the vast majority of teachers do not understand their role in this area of work, but worse still that other professionals do not understand the particular role of teachers'.

Since then there have been various developments designed to address these concerns. Child abuse inquiries, such as those detailed above, clearly highlighted the need for improved co-ordination of this work and were instrumental in every local authority setting up Area Review Committees, which subsequently became known as Area Child Protection Committees (ACPCs). Amongst the duties of ACPCs are the establishment, maintenance and review of local inter-agency guidelines on procedures to be followed in individual cases; the scrutiny of arrangements in relation to inter-agency liaison and the monitoring and scrutiny of work related to inter-agency training. The duty of local authorities, education authorities, housing authorities and health authorities to co-operate in their functions to support children and families is set out in Section 27 of the Children Act 1989.

Measures designed to clarify and support the school's role also emerged from the then Department of Education and Science (DES) and subsequently the Department for Education and Employment (DfEE). The Beckford inquiry (1985) emphasised the importance of the school as part of the management of the child abuse system and recommended the appointment of a designated child protection teacher in every school, which was subsequently adopted in governmental guidelines. Circular 4/88 (DES, 1988) recommended that 'a senior member of a school's staff should have responsibility, under the procedures established by the Local Education Authority (LEA), for co-ordinating action within the school and for liaison with other agencies'. Some seven years later Circular 10/95 (DfEE, 1995) set out the responsibility for child protection issues within education departments, schools and colleges and gave guidance on links with other agencies involved in the protection of children. Each LEA was directed to appoint a senior official to have overall responsibility for the co-ordination of policy, procedures and training **and** for making sure that procedures are set out in authority-wide documentation. The guidelines also reinforced the recommendation that all schools have a senior member of staff as the designated and named child protection liaison teacher/co-ordinator who has been adequately trained.

Another key development was the Home Office document *Working Together Under the Children Act, 1989* (Home Office et al, 1991) where the key role of schools in protecting children from abuse was recognised:

Because of their day-to-day contact with individual children during school terms, teachers and other school staff are particularly well placed to observe outward signs of abuse, changes in behaviour or failure to thrive.

The clear message from *Working Together* was that action will be most effective when taken in collaboration with other agencies.

Earlier research

However, very little attention has been paid to assessing the impact which schools have made in this area. In *Child Abuse Trends in England and Wales 1983-1987* (Creighton and Noyes, 1989) the authors reported teachers' declining role in the system, despite the increase in school age children on the Child Protection Register. Although Maher (1987) regarded teachers as important identifiers of sexual abuse, uncovering 35% of those who do become known, he went on to estimate that an average comprehensive school may expect to contain 80 sexually abused students which, he suggested, leaves three-quarters unidentified. However, all this was before the initiatives introduced from 1988 onwards.

It is clear that the vast majority of schools and LEAs have established the required structures and procedures in line with the guidelines (see Chapter 3), but it is still not clear how effective these have been in improving the identification and prevention of child abuse. Although Elliott (1996) has expressed his concern about the low rate of referral from schools, his study was conducted within one Education and Library Board in Northern Ireland and in discussions with the author he has emphasised the impact which sectarian troubles have had on this process.

Kirkland, Field and Hazel (1996) report their own experience, which is that knowledge of child protection procedures and an awareness of the issues have not reached all staff in schools, and express their concerns about the implications of this. Evidence which they have gathered indicates that the larger the school in terms of staff and pupil numbers, and the higher the staff turnover, the more serious the problem becomes. Their bleak conclusion is that it is '... likely that in many of the country's schools abused children are not being identified and dealt with in a manner which is consistent with the law and locally agreed procedures'. It is not apparent to what extent this is due to the pressures which have been on schools in recent years to respond to so many requirements imposed by government. It is possible that some have resorted to meeting the bare requirements, particularly in those areas of children's lives which are not directly associated with their place in public examination league tables or expanding or maintaining the student number on roll. All in all it paints a rather confused picture of what is actually going on. But it is evident that many schools are faced with ever increasing concerns about students in their care and that they do not always feel they have the adequate expertise, support or resources to begin to address the problems.

There will be difficulties associated with inter-agency communications and the gap which arises when translating theoretical understanding of child protection into effective practice. Zellman (1990) interviewed child protection staff in six states in the USA and found that teachers often irritated other professionals because of their high referral rate. Teachers were said to report cases which were not sufficiently serious to trigger a high priority response. Yet teachers had been drawn into the child protection process because of the belief that they would be able to pick up early signs of abuse before they become serious. Other US studies had indicated that teachers there generally have a poor reporting rate. In this country teachers have been said to be on the periphery of the child protection process (see Birchall and Hallett, 1995). This was on the basis of work carried out in the early 1990s, soon after the introduction of the Children Act 1989 and the DES circular 4/88 (Department for Education and Employment, 1988) which began to specify and clarify the role of education in the child protection process. Schools should now be playing a major role in the referral process. The responses received from schools in the survey reported in Chapter 3 show very little reluctance on their part to be involved in this process but there are evident strains, some compounded by failure of communication and perceived lack of support. Both would indicate that Birchall and Hallett's assertion that schools are not well integrated into the network continues to be true.

There are clearly other issues which demand an examination. One author has recently described as a 'chasm' the divide which too often exists between schools and teachers on the one hand and the non-educational services to children on the other (Gilligan, 1998). He goes on to quote Jackson's (1994) observation on '… the deep split between education and care which runs through all our institutions and services for children'.

Earlier studies perhaps provide some clues as to why this is the case or, at least, why it continues to exist despite structures and policies which should ease inter-professional liaison. Birchall and Hallett (1995) surveyed the experience and perceptions of the six key professions involved in child protection work. In the course of this study the views of 81 teachers were obtained. On the basis of their responses the authors conclude that:

Some teachers might welcome and undertake a pastoral role but not all see this as an appropriate function or compatible with their primary pedagogic responsibilities for a class.

They speculate that this viewpoint may become increasingly common:

…with recent policy developments, including Local Management of Schools, the concentration on targets of attainment and a more competitive atmosphere in the education system.

These factors seem to have attained even greater significance in the years since that was written.

The same authors stress the importance of inter-professional co-operation at all stages of the child protection process and draw attention to what they see as a major impediment to achieving this:

Nearly everyone [of the key professions involved in child protection work] but the police deems teachers' role important or essential but significant numbers find teachers difficult to co-operate with…. There is evidently a large unresolved question [about the role of the teachers]. They appear to be well placed to identify and refer children to the specialist agencies but clearly are not well integrated into the network.

Another important area which was identified in Birchall and Hallett's work was that of the difficulty involved in arriving at a consensual definition of referral thresholds, leaving some schools confused by Social Services' failure to intervene in cases (or to carry out an initial investigation and decide that further action was not required) where a child protection issue had been identified and reported. This is an area to which Murphy (1995) has also drawn attention. He calls it the 'double bind' present in the British system whereby different definitions of what is serious abuse can lead to child protection referrals from the Education Service not being properly processed or not being made in the first place:

Successful referrals rely, to a large extent, on educational personnel understanding the definition of 'significant harm' which is used by the main processing agency – the Social Services Department.

Some light has been thrown on this area by Hallett's study of inter-agency co-ordination in child protection (Hallett, 1995), although it also indicated that, despite Government recommendations, little had changed since Maher's pessimistic observation. A questionnaire sent to members of the main professions involved in this work found that teachers, together with general practitioners, headed the list of those whose roles were 'very unclear' or 'rather unclear'. The same author interviewed a sample of teachers, along with representatives of the other professions, and uncovered considerable variation in the extent to which teachers were familiar with the inter-agency referral procedures and the local procedural guidelines. Birchall's (1992) study had also found a high level of uncertainty amongst teachers about their own role. They scored the highest of all professions with 29% considering that they were rather or very unclear about their own role in child protection cases. Dr Dorit Braun has also claimed that while teachers do care a great deal about child protection issues there were considerable obstacles to their further participation, not least the need to become absolutely clear and confident about their role before they could be expected to contribute to work across the agencies (see Michael Sieff Foundation, 1994). In a study conducted by Campbell and Wigglesworth (1993), despite finding that knowledge of signs of child abuse was found to be good in the great majority of cases, 40% of the 142 teachers surveyed in an area of Scotland were neither confident of recognising these signs nor of responding appropriately if approached by a child with signs of abuse.

Educational context

There have been other developments which have had a significant impact on this work. No one has yet established the consequences of the increased fragmentation of the educational services, with the possibility that Local Management of Schools and grant maintained status may have reduced the co-ordinating role of Local Education Authorities (Barker, 1996). In a situation increasingly subject to market forces, more schools are competing for pupils, particularly those who are seen to carry a higher chance of achieving academic success and a lower risk of requiring additional resources or support. Hinchcliffe (1993) carried out a survey of child protection systems and concluded that:

Fifty per cent of the 48 authorities responding said that they feared the introduction of Local Management of Schools (LMS)…would weaken the child protection service.

One respondent claimed:

Power is now so diffused we cannot negotiate individually with head teachers, governors, education department staff – it is frequently impossible to see how schools reluctant to abide by agreed procedures and good child protection practice can be forced to do so.

Other significant changes have also occurred with the transfer of responsibility from LEAs to the Office for Standards in Education (OFSTED) for the inspection of child protection policies in schools and with the changing nature of the Education Welfare Service in many parts of the country.

The need for research

Research is clearly needed to shed light on the day-to-day realities of schools' involvement in the child protection process. NSPCC intends to undertake such research. It would allow many of the strands which have been examined individually to be studied in a co-ordinated way and provide practitioners, policy makers and researchers with a clearer understanding of the role of the education service (after a period of considerable change), in relation to child protection, than is available at the present time. As a prelude to this it was important to identify how schools and LEAs were approaching the area of child protection and to begin to examine the training which teachers receive to prepare and support them in this work. A survey of all teacher training institutions in England and Wales collected information on the amount of time which was devoted to child protection, as well as on the content of this input and the attitude of tutors to the subject. Alongside this all LEAs in England and Wales were surveyed to determine how they were supporting schools to carry out their responsibilities in the area of child protection; and a sample of schools that had previously responded to a questionnaire sent out by NSPCC were recontacted to collect their views on how they were meeting these responsibilities. The results of this stage of the research are reported in the chapters which follow.

2 Child protection training in initial teacher training: results of a preliminary survey

Background

As examined in Chapter 1 there is now a growing literature on child abuse in relation to education and educational programmes. Most concern has focused on the meaning, recognition and socio-cultural context of abuse, its prevalence within the family over time and across cultures (see for example Jenks, 1996) and its detection and prevention within social institutions, including schools. Pressure for change and intervention in professional training did accelerate and this has been reflected to some extent in practice. Following the recommendations of a number of high profile cases professional training programmes are offered to carers and to relevant medical and social welfare personnel.

While the significance of the teacher's role in child protection has long been recognised, it is only relatively recently that specific relevant training has been proposed. In the mid-eighties a number of authors advocated a major extension of such work into the professional training of teachers, but the emphasis was on experienced teachers. With the appearance of Circular 4/88 (Department of Education and Science, 1988) the responsibility of the various parts of the education system became clear and this was quickly followed by the 1989 Children Act, which had a significant impact on professional practices relating to children. Another section of this book examines the response which LEAs made to these various initiatives. It is evident that most LEAs have made considerable efforts to ensure that teachers with designated responsibility for child protection issues in schools have received some training, and to a lesser extent to raise the awareness of the wider body of teachers. Far less attention has been paid to students training to be teachers.

As the results of the survey, reported later in this chapter, show many courses have included some relevant teaching, the adequacy of which is open to debate. But it was not until 1996 that specific coverage of child protection issues was discussed as a future requirement on initial teacher training (ITT) courses. Subsequently Circular 4/98 *Teaching: High Status, High Standards* (Department for Education and Employment, 1998) laid down the Secretary of State for Education and Employment's requirements for all ITT courses. There is one standard in the new ITT curriculum which relates directly to child protection and this states that:

...for all courses, those to be awarded Qualified Teacher Status should, when assessed, demonstrate that they have a working knowledge and understanding of teachers' legal liabilities and responsibilities.

These liabilities and responsibilities are those specified in Circular 10/95 (Department for Education and Employment, 1995) and in *Working Together: a guide to arrangements for inter-agency co-operation for the protection of children from abuse, 1991* (Home Office et al.,1991). This study was completed before these requirements were implemented, although courses and schools involved in training teachers were aware of the earlier set of draft recommendations which were very similar to the final version.

For more than a decade teacher education has been undergoing radical change. More time is now spent in schools and less in the institutions. Training for competencies, defined as specific and very detailed skills and subject knowledge, is the dominant driving force and in the view of many teacher educators this has greatly reduced the significance of generic 'Educational Studies' which previously would have included child development. Primary courses are now required to devote 150 hours to each of the three core subjects of the National Curriculum thus creating particular pressures on time. The National Curriculum for ITT emphasises National Curriculum based subject knowledge and although other areas are clearly present in Circular 4/98 (Department for Education and Employment, 1998) those that deal with issues of child welfare are not accorded equal status with their academic counterparts. In the opinion of many the very notion of teacher education is being lost to the more instrumental vision implied in teacher training.

The survey

The survey[1] was conducted against this background with the intention of providing some base data on what was happening on ITT courses as far as input in relation to child protection was concerned. Early in the autumn term 1997 a questionnaire and explanatory letter were sent to all higher education institutions providing ITT according to the Universities Council for the Education of Teachers (UCET) (Appendix A). The UCET list did not specify individual courses and so multiple copies were sent to each institutional contact named by UCET, although the intention was that they would be passed to the most appropriate person to try to ensure coverage of all relevant courses within each institution. In the event 128 replies were received from 68 institutions (82% of institutions providing ITT courses at that time). Sixty-two per cent of these courses were Post Graduate Certificate in Education courses (PGCEs), 22% were either BA or BSc courses with a teaching qualification, 15% were BEds and 1% were Master of Education courses. Because of the high proportion of PGCEs the majority of courses lasted for one year, 12% were three-year courses and 22% were four-year courses. Fifty-nine per cent of the courses were designed to prepare students to teach in the primary sector, 37% were aimed at the secondary sector and 4% were described as preparation for teaching in upper primary/lower secondary schools. Most of the questionnaires (61%) were completed by the course co-ordinator/leader, with 23% by heads of department, 6% by senior tutors and 10% by other members of the teaching teams. The questionnaire consisted of a combination of closed questions concerned with course provision and open questions eliciting explanatory and reflective comments.

The same questionnaire and a covering letter was sent to the newer school-based training courses, School Centred Initial Teacher Training courses (SCITTs). SCITTs were introduced in 1993 as an alternative route to achieving qualified teacher status. Based on consortia of schools the intention is to provide the opportunity to design, organise and provide school-based courses for graduates. At the time when the survey was sent out 26 consortia were providing such courses, covering both primary and secondary sectors. The questionnaire was addressed to the managers in these consortia. Fourteen of the 26 replied, representing a 54% response rate, which is considerably below that received from the courses based in higher education institutions. This relatively low return rate, combined with issues emerging from the questionnaires which were returned, led to the decision to try to interview those who had replied. Each of the responding SCITTs managers was approached with such a request to which they all agreed.[2]

---

[1] The research was jointly conducted by the author and Keith Hodgkinson, Senior Lecturer in the Education Department at Loughborough University.

[2] The interviews were conducted by the researchers involved in the study.

Child protection input on higher education courses

The overwhelming majority (118, 92%)[3] of responding higher education courses claimed to have an element dedicated to child protection issues, with 115 of these courses reporting that it was a compulsory part. However, this means that ten courses, of which seven were PGCE courses, had no coverage.

Course content and design

Most courses (66%) cover it after the first assessed school placement, with the rest almost equally spread between courses doing so before this placement and those covering it after the final placement. A very small number of courses did make some provision for coverage during a placement.

Respondents were asked to say how long was spent on the child protection element. Most courses offered more than one hour, but it was just one hour or less on 17% of courses. One course offered an eight-hour element, but this was part of a more general conference on child protection and related issues. Perhaps surprisingly there was no significant difference between the length of the input on PGCE courses and that on the longer degree courses. For five courses, labelled as 'Other', categorisation presented difficulties. In some cases this was because the students were given directed tasks related to the subject to complete on their placements or they were presented with a combination of workshops, seminars and lectures which varied from year to year. In addition to the time allocations presented in the table, six courses also had optional modules related to child protection that would then enable students to extend their coverage of the subject. (The results are recorded in Figure 1.)

The respondents were then asked about the content of the child protection input, shown in Table 1. Most courses appeared to be meeting the requirements that were subsequently set out in Circular 4/98 (Department for Education and Employment, 1998).

---

[3] The figures are now percentages of the courses covering child protection issues.

Figure 1 Length of child protection element

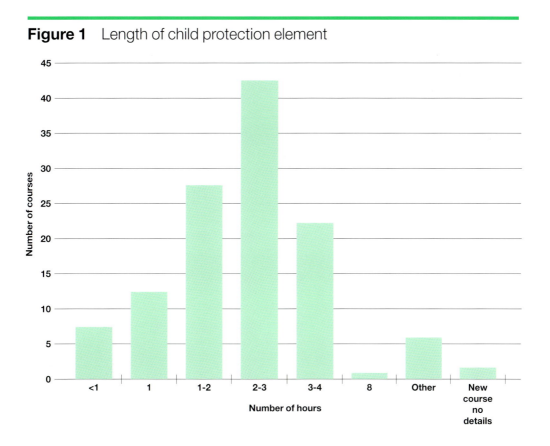

Table 1 Content of child protection input on ITT courses in higher
education institutions

Content	Percentage of courses offering coverage
School procedures for dealing with suspected abuse	97
Detection of children at risk	87
Agencies involved in child protection cases	87
Children Act 1989	85
Incidence of child protection cases in schools	69
Incidence of child protection cases in society	53
Discussion of case studies	52
Other issues	19

Of the 22 courses giving details of other issues, nine included the relationship of child protection to teaching and learning; ten related it to behaviour management and five linked child protection with school policies. Four courses opened up a discussion of personal experience, three explored the dangers of getting a child protection decision wrong and one wove it in with an explanation of the UN Convention on Rights of the Child. However, only a third of courses either set or recommended relevant reading material.

Over 80% of these courses were taught by, or had some input from, an outside speaker. Most of these were social workers, but head teachers and other senior teachers were frequent presenters. Other professionals involved in this work included specialists from Local Education Authorities, the Police, NSPCC, and the Probation Service. Very few courses were currently using their own staff to teach this subject but there was certainly some concern amongst respondents about how they would be able to continue to meet the costs of outside speakers and comments which indicated that they may have to consider providing it themselves.

Most providing courses deploy a combination of teaching strategies. Ninety-five per cent of courses deal with this subject in lectures, 57% use discussion groups, 42% use workshops, and 29% cover the issue in seminars. Ten courses said they used distance learning materials with six of them setting assessed assignments on the basis of these. Overall about a third of courses either set or recommended reading material on the subject. However, only 12% assessed any work which students completed on child protection.

The impact of changes in requirements on ITT courses

Those responding to the questionnaire were asked to assess the possible long term effects on their courses in the light of the requirements of the earlier Circular 10/97 and the later Circular 4/98 (Department for Education and Employment, 1998) and their Welsh equivalents. As explained earlier in this chapter these regulations specify, in some considerable detail, both the content of teacher training courses and the skills and competencies expected of newly qualified members of the teaching profession. Well over half of the courses did not think that the new provisions would make any difference to what was taught in relation to child protection, with 31% estimating that there would be an overall increase. There were some concerns expressed that because of the very prescriptive nature of the curriculum for ITT courses and the breadth of material which had to be covered, the opportunities for extending their input on child protection would be severely limited and, in some cases, it could even be reduced. There were courses that attempted to give students a greater understanding of the subject whose organisers feared they may have to restrict their teaching to the minimum requirements of the Teacher Training Agency.

Courses without any child protection training

Ten courses, of which seven were PGCE courses, did not cover child protection at all. In one instance the respondent came from a new course where its final shape had not yet been decided and so it was possible that it may still have been introduced. Three of the others claimed that it was not covered because the present curriculum was so overloaded that it did not leave any opportunity to do so. A further four thought that the content of the core professional studies and special needs courses alerted their students to related issues, making any additional input unnecessary. Two respondents thought that it was inappropriate as their students would be working with senior teachers. However, of these ten, seven said they did want to include relevant teaching on their courses, two were firmly against any such move and one reluctantly acknowledged the inevitability of needing to conform with the standards required of newly qualified teachers (NQTs).

At the end of the questionnaire respondents were invited to add any comments which they wished to make about the coverage of child protection on ITT courses. Certain patterns clearly emerge in these comments which are worthy of note. A minority of respondents displayed a very strong commitment to the subject of child protection; they were anxious to maintain its quality and were confident that what they were doing was of a high quality. Many more gave the impression that they were attempting to meet their responsibilities in this area amidst many difficulties. One third of respondents specifically mentioned the time pressures on ITT courses to fit in every requirement and balanced this against comments about the complex nature of child protection and the near impossibility of adequately covering the subject with students. Other constraints referred to were the lack of clear guidance on what should be covered, alongside the lack of relevant expertise within ITT departments which meant paying for outside lecturers at a time when funding was barely adequate.

Child protection input on SCITT courses

Of the fourteen responses received from SCITTs, ten claimed to have a child protection element. Of the four not dealing with the issue at all, one respondent said their course was still evolving and the other three did not think it required any dedicated sessions.

Most of the courses covered the subject very early on in the autumn term. The time devoted to the subject varied considerably. Four courses spent three to four hours on child protection, one spent one to two hours, two spent two hours and three courses reported spending less than one hour on the subject. The teaching styles adopted were similar to those in higher education institutions. Six schemes used a school teacher or head teacher and four used a specialist, although in the questionnaire there were no details provided about the specialisms that they held.

All the courses claimed to cover the Children Act and the detection of children at risk; eight included input on procedures and eight dealt with the agencies which are responsible for dealing with abuse; five dealt with the incidence of child protection in schools and two with the incidence in society in general. However, some of the additional comments made by respondents indicated that there were possibly areas of concern that had not emerged in the answers to the closed questions. Examples of such comments were:

NQTs would be inducted into the right way of doing things once they are in schools. How much do trainees need to know in advance?

We deal with it in passing rather than as a separate specific issue.

The nature of these and other responses, as well as the relatively low return rate led to the decision to interview all SCITTs managers who had responded.

The responses from SCITTs had indicated some degree of uncertainty on the part of those running these courses about what they should be covering on child protection issues and this was borne out in face-to-face contact with them. With the exception of one primary course and one secondary course the coverage emerged as extremely patchy. In some cases there was an extraordinarily high level of uncertainty, and in some cases alarm, about the content while in others there was an almost casual approach to the issue with comments such as:

We thought of it late and just stuck it in.

and

If I am to be honest and think through our professional component of the course we are not specifically targeting it…it will come up in a haphazard manner.

For the most part the approach tended to be one of permeation rather than planned modules or sessions. Most managers had focused what coverage there was on teachers' legal and professional responsibilities. In many cases, they were reluctant to go beyond the minimum requirements, usually out of fear that students may be upset or confronted by their own memories or out of a desire to adopt realistic goals for ITT and leave further development to the schools employing the NQTs. In general, quite considerable expectations were laid at the door of these schools to develop their trainees' experience in relation to child protection, although the study did not follow up the schools to see to what extent they were aware of these expectations.

As far as the permeation model is concerned differences did emerge between primary and secondary sector SCITTs as to where the child protection related areas were covered. The primary ones were more likely to do this in the few sessions devoted to child development, whereas in the secondary SCITTs it was more often linked to physical education and/or bullying.

During two of these interviews the SCITTs managers invited the researchers to meet their trainees. One group comprised students from a primary course and a secondary course run by the same SCITT, while the other was in the secondary sector. Although this provided an opportunity to begin to examine the issue with trainees, the issues that emerged need to be discussed with a wider audience to assess how representative their experiences are. The students on the secondary course remembered that the subject was mentioned in the pastoral care segment and although they recalled there having been scenarios their memories were limited to one involving a child with 'smelly feet'. They also recalled references to the teacher's role and responsibilities were covered but no one could remember specific details. Although they had completed their school placements at the time of the discussion neither could anyone remember any discussion having taken place with school staff on the subject nor had any of them been told which member of staff was the designated teacher with responsibility for child protection issues.

If anything the experience of interviewing the mixed primary and secondary group was more disturbing. Not only were they even less informed about the issue but there was also a large degree of scepticism about a school's and a teacher's part in the process. There was a general agreement that their views on child protection owed more to reports in the media, and particularly in tabloid newspapers, than to their courses.

As the discussions proceeded it was evident that trainees in both groups had come across a range of situations involving child protection concerns, but in only one case had there been any intervention. This was an incident when a student had disclosed that she was being abused at home and a trainee had taken her to the school nurse's office while she (the trainee) found out about the procedures. In another case a student had been alarmed by a child's behaviour and reports of what happened at home and had reported these concerns to his mentor, but as far as he was aware no further action had been taken.

Discussion

It is worth remembering that this survey and the accompanying interviews were conducted before the introduction of the requirements contained in Circular 4/98 *Teaching: High Status, High Standards* (Department for Education and Employment, 1998) which sets down the Secretary of State for Education and Employment's requirements for all ITT courses. But alongside this was the finding that well over half of the courses did not think that the new provisions would make any difference to what was taught in relation to child protection, with only 31% assessing that there would be an overall increase. Most courses were already offering more the minimum required to comply with the Government's standard. It seems unlikely that without a clear commitment on the part of Government to raising the profile of child protection on ITT courses even those courses which believed there would be an overall increase will be faced by the pressures to meet the many other demands being made on them and will continue to provide minimal input. The majority of respondents were not satisfied with the level of their provision and would have preferred to have offered more, but time was not available. ITT courses have clearly become standards-related and have moved away from the more rounded notion of 'education'. Harris (1994) is just one commentator who has pointed to the negative effects of teacher training reforms on students' learning, attitudes and professional development. It is questionable to what extent such a factual knowledge-based approach on its own can produce teachers capable of assuming responsibility for, and understanding of, the complexities of child protection. Teacher educators pointed with regret to the disappearance of a significant input on child development, because with its demise a further opportunity for students to reflect on child protection issues had gone, along with the opportunity to gain knowledge of what may be regarded as 'normal' against which the signs and symptoms of abuse could be measured.

Very few courses made any provision for the systematic treatment of the issues on placements. Neither was there a consensus on the most effective time for dealing with child protection. There is clearly a place for some guidance on how best to contribute to, and build on, students' developing exposure to the realities of teaching and pupil management, but this may require some preliminary research to determine the optimum time for teaching about child protection and for then assessing its effectiveness.

Given that the content of the child protection element also varied considerably and that only a third of courses either set or recommended reading materials it is probable that many would welcome some guidance on these issues. In order to meet the requirements demanded of ITT courses and to address the concerns of some about what should be included and how to cope if they are not able to continue to pay for outside experts to teach, it is likely that many courses would welcome detailed guidance on what should be covered, together with appropriate support materials and even specialist input from other agencies able to support these courses on a voluntary basis. This may in turn help to raise the profile of the subject on courses and contribute to the continuing professional development of the next generation of teachers. All this would, however, depend on time being available on courses. While time was clearly a major stumbling block, as most courses currently devote some time to child protection such a move may allow them to make optimum use of that time and, possibly, link with other related subject areas.

Interviews with the managers of SCITTs focused attention on a number of issues that may have implications for courses in the higher education sector. Although there were a few SCITTs that seemed to have a well-informed conception of their role which they appeared to be translating into reality, most were providing minimal coverage of child protection issues and had not attempted to relate it to a more rounded professional approach. It was surprising that despite the fact that these courses were based in schools the designated teachers with responsibility for child protection were rarely involved in sharing their experience or expertise.

There was a degree of uncertainty on SCITT courses about whether to adopt a 'bolt on' child protection element or develop a model akin to permeation. Most had opted for the latter, using a combination of items on child development, pastoral responsibilities and special educational needs. Such a model, however, requires a considerable degree of planning and monitoring to ensure that all the essential elements are covered and this did not appear to be happening.

The interviews did uncover evidence amongst the trainees of ignorance and serious misconceptions about the nature and incidence of child abuse, and in some cases this was reflected in the observations made by their trainers. However, there is no reason to believe that child protection input on the SCITTs that were examined was any worse than that on most higher education courses. It was just that the opportunity to examine the former in greater detail was available. There is a great deal to be done to address these shortcomings if children are to receive the support and assistance they deserve.

Although the acquisition of factually-based information on child protection is now compulsory, the sheer volume of compulsory elements together with the emphasis on curriculum knowledge leaves very little opportunity to devote the time needed to cover a very important and complex subject. Not only has knowledge to be transmitted but so frequently people's assumptions and misconceptions need to be challenged. It is a daunting task but one that may be achievable if those entrusted with preparing the next generation of teachers are given appropriate and high-quality support.

But it is also worth considering what is realistic to expect of ITT courses. Everything known about learning indicates that without experience of the subject and the opportunity to put what is taught into practice knowledge will not become embedded. This is certainly not to argue that providers should do nothing. Rather, what is done should be linked systematically to the students' experience on teaching practice and then to their induction year. College and university staff, mentors, designated teachers and other appropriate professionals need to work together, but to do so they may well need support and appropriate materials, as well as an awareness of each other's responsibilities and a recognition that one sector cannot, and should not, work in isolation.

3 Schools' responses to child protection

Background to the survey

In 1994 NSPCC published an updated version of *Protecting Children – A Guide for Teachers on Child Abuse*. The purpose of the booklet was to help teachers identify abuse and to provide them with an understanding of how abused children may feel and react at a time of crisis. A questionnaire was included in those sent out during the first three months following publication with the intention of obtaining feedback on the content and design of the booklet and any concerns which teachers may have had about their responsibilities in the child protection process. Four hundred and twenty responses were received from schools in England, Northern Ireland and Wales, 68% of which came from teachers working in the primary sector and 32% from secondary teachers. Ninety-five per cent of the schools were in the state sector (92% being locally managed and 3% grant maintained).

It was evident that these schools took their responsibilities in this area very seriously and had endeavoured to meet the recommendations set out in Circular 4/88 *Working Together for the Protection of Children from Abuse: Procedures Within the Education Service* issued by the then Department of Education and Science in 1988. At that time all but ten of the 420 schools said they had a designated teacher with responsibility for child protection and 94% had procedures in place for responding to child abuse. But there was a range of issues with which schools were grappling. The main concerns which were expressed about the teacher's role in child protection and prevention of child abuse were:

- the role of schools in case conferences
- the ability of teachers to recognise signs of abuse
- parent/teacher relationships
- supporting staff when dealing with child protection issues
- the lack of effective communication between agencies
- the lack of experience/training in this area of most staff
- supporting children who have been abused
- dealing with children who have been abused
- lack of time to get to know students
- uncertainties about contacting Social Services
- time involved in dealing with child protection issues.

In the autumn of 1997 a further questionnaire was sent to all these respondents. A decision was taken to exclude the respondents in Northern Ireland from this phase of the research as different government directives apply there. This meant that 385 questionnaires were sent out. Since the previous questionnaire the Department for Education and Employment (1995) issued Circular 10/95 which contains further guidance on child protection procedures in educational settings. It updates and revises previous guidance given in the Department of Education and Science Circular 4/88 and one intention of the questionnaire was to examine the extent to which its main recommendations had been implemented, although many schools had adopted these before this Circular appeared.

The circular makes it clear that LEAs and schools have responsibilities in relation to child protection and states that:

- All staff should be alert to signs of abuse and know to whom they should report any concerns or suspicions

- All schools and colleges should have a designated member of staff responsible for co-ordinating action within the institution and liaising with other agencies, including the Area Child Protection Committees (ACPCs)

- All schools and colleges should be aware of child protection procedures established by the ACPC and, where appropriate, by the LEA

- All schools and colleges should have procedures, which all staff should be aware of, for dealing with cases of suspected and actual child abuse, including any accusations against members of staff

- The member of staff with designated responsibility for child protection in a school or college should receive appropriate training

- In every LEA a senior officer should be responsible for co-ordinating child protection interventions across the LEA.

The survey and respondents

The questionnaires were sent out in early November 1997 and most were returned by the deadline in early December, although a subsequent reminder brought returns into early 1998. In all, 327 replies were received which represents 85% of those distributed. Eighty-seven per cent of these 327 questionnaires contained the name of the respondent and the school. Over half (57%) of the questionnaires were completed by the same person who had made the initial response in 1994.

Sixty-three per cent of the replies were from schools in the primary sector, 34% from the secondary sector, 2% were from middle schools and the remaining 1% from all-age schools in the independent sector. Overall 96% of the schools were in the State sector (5% of which were grant maintained).

By far the largest proportion of questionnaires was completed by head teachers. Overall this was 58%, but with a far higher proportion in the primary sector (91% compared with 7% from secondary schools), which probably reflects the differences in the sectors in relation to the posts held by the designated teacher with responsibility for child protection (to be referred to in this report as the designated teacher). Twenty-one per cent of responses came from deputy head teachers, 9% from senior teachers and 5% from special needs co-ordinators in schools. The remaining 7% were completed by other members of the schools' staff, most of whom had some responsibility for child protection. Overall 90% of the persons completing the questionnaire were the designated teacher with responsibility for child protection in their schools.

Designated teachers

All but one of the 327 responding schools had a designated teacher. The one exception was a state primary school. In 50% of schools this was the head teacher, although there was a significant difference between primary and secondary schools. In 93% of primary schools the head teacher was also the designated teacher, while in the secondary sector the figure was 10%. Secondary schools were far more likely to have appointed a deputy head teacher into the designated role (65% compared with 4% in primary schools). Most primary school teachers spend their school hours in front of a class and non-contact time is virtually nonexistent. While it is increasingly being encroached on in secondary schools, the fact that there are more teachers in secondary schools provides a level of flexibility which may allow teachers to be released to attend out-of-school meetings. In primary schools it may only be feasible for a head teacher to leave the school premises during the school day. In a minority of schools it fell to a senior teacher or to the special needs co-ordinator or to another assigned teacher. In 8% of schools there was more than one designated teacher, although this was twice as likely in the primary schools in the study.

Child protection policies

Circular 10/95 (Department for Education and Employment, 1995) emphasises the importance of schools developing a child protection policy with which members of staff should be familiar. The policy should cover:

- procedures for dealing with cases

- links with other agencies

- guidance on handling information

- the support which should be available to pupils

- details of appropriate training.

The overwhelming majority of schools (94%) have a child protection policy in place and 99% have established procedures, in accordance with their policies and/or those of their LEAs.

School governors and child protection

Governors are responsible for ensuring that the school has a child protection policy and a designated member of staff for child protection. There is no specific recommendation that a school should have a governor with such responsibility and only 27% of the responding schools had such a governor.

OFSTED and child protection

The Office for Standards in Education (OFSTED) requires its inspectors to make a judgement about a school's ability to promote the welfare, health, safety and guidance of its pupils. Inspectors need to look at child protection policies and procedures to decide if they conform to the guidance given by the DfEE and establish that the schools comply with this guidance by:

- having a designated member of staff

- following local ACPC procedures

- liaising with other agencies involved in child protection

- taking part in appropriate training.

At the time of the survey most of the schools had been inspected by OFSTED (83% of all state schools) or by HM Inspectorate (4 of the 12 independent schools). The questionnaire sought information about the extent to which child protection figured in these inspections. In all sectors and phases there were respondents who were not able to answer certain questions, mainly because they had not been in post at the time of the inspection.

Of the 263 schools that had received an OFSTED inspection, 63% were sure that the policy had been inspected by their OFSTED teams; 11% were sure that it had not been, 16% did not know and in 10% of schools no policy had been in place at the time of the inspection. They were also asked if the inspectors' reports had commented on the child protection policy. Thirty-nine per cent of responses from the inspected schools said the report did contain such comments, but 53% said there were no relevant comments in their reports. (Eight per cent did not know, which is perhaps surprising as the report would still be available and 10% did not have a policy at the inspection.) For the period autumn 1992 to summer 1996 approximately one-third of reports on schools in the study were said to contain a comment on child protection policies, but of those schools inspected in 1996/1997 it was claimed that 53% did, which may reflect an increasing awareness about this issue after the appearance of Circular 10/95, or it may have come with more experienced inspectors and an increased awareness of the importance of including a comment in the report.

In only 27% of inspections was the policy discussed with the head teacher and in 43% of cases it was discussed with the designated teacher. In 20% of inspections it was known that discussions had taken place with other members of staff to assess their awareness of the child protection policies and procedures current in their schools, and similar discussions had taken place with support staff in 10% of inspections. In 6% of inspections discussions had taken place with the chairpersons of the governing bodies and/or with the governor with responsibility for child protection.

In only 5 of the 263 inspections were discussions about child protection policies and procedures known to have occurred with anyone else and these included a discussion at a meeting between the inspectors and parents, with another unspecified governor, with lunch time supervisors ('dinner ladies') and school administrative staff. It is important to note that such discussions may have taken place during other inspections without the respondent being aware of them.

Other areas explored in the survey

The research also set out to explore in more detail issues which had been covered in the earlier survey. A range of concerns had been expressed in that study about schools' role in relation to child protection. They were included in this questionnaire to:

■ see if they were still current concerns

■ attempt to gauge the level of concern that existed

■ obtain views on the agencies which they thought would give the most appropriate support.

Case conferences

Some schools had expressed concern or uncertainty about how best to be represented at case conferences. Of the 327 schools in the study, 93% (305) said they would usually be represented at case conferences and there were many comments which indicated a real willingness to be involved and an appreciation of the importance of a school's perspective being represented. With only one exception, which was a school where a representative would never be sent, the remaining 21 schools had never been approached to attend a conference. In those schools which had experience of case conferences and with head teachers who were also designated teachers with responsibility for child protection, 88% would always attend or would do so on most occasions, with 11% sometimes attending. Only 9% of head teachers who were not designated teachers always attended case conferences or did so on most occasions; a further 13% sometimes did so.

Others attending case conferences:

■ 53% of designated teachers (other than head teachers who were designated teachers) always or mostly did so and 39% sometimes did

■ 41% of heads of year in secondary schools always or mostly attended case conferences and a further 45% sometimes went

■ only 8% of form teachers always or mostly attended case conferences, with 36% sometimes attending, with no significant differences between primary and secondary schools

■ a range of involved individuals such as special needs co-ordinators (3% of schools), classroom assistants, a school nurse, individual tutors and others who were seen to be appropriate in particular circumstances.

Of the 305 schools with experience of child protection conferences 85% of schools said they were able to provide written reports for case conferences.

While most schools had no difficulty in deciding which member of staff should attend the conference, 11% of schools admitted that they did. Their problems focused on two areas:

■ the decision about whether or not to send the person seen to be the most appropriate even if this would create problems for the school or the teacher, typified by these replies from head teachers:

I would like class teachers to attend – they know the children better than anyone here – but there are problems about curriculum continuity, paying for cover and disrupting the other children's experience.

As the head teacher I feel confident when I attend and represent the school. A teacher may well know the child better than I do but it could be a much more daunting experience for a class teacher.

■ the decision about which of two or more teachers, both or all deemed to be equally appropriate, should attend :

Sometimes the form teacher will know pupils very well, but the head of year does as well. We cannot afford to release two members of staff and often I [head teacher] attend because I have more experience of conferences, but then that becomes self-perpetuating.

Half of the schools (51%) said they often received what they considered to be inadequate notice of conferences. It is clearly difficult to co-ordinate the very different work schedules of the professionals involved in these events. But the lack of flexibility within school timetables creates real problems if insufficient notice is given as these comments indicate:

The date is always fixed without reference to school events which are very difficult to change and sometimes it is difficult to spend time in case conferences, however important the circumstances.

We usually get late notice of these conferences and when we go along we are not necessarily as prepared as we should be.

The same proportion said they did not receive full information about the cases under discussion at these conferences. It was evident from the replies that many schools thought that some Social Services Departments could often make more effort to share relevant information before the conference:

We often do not get any information prior to the conference about particular issues, so we feel unsure about what we will have to face and/or what additional information it might be useful for us to supply.

Our experience has been that all too often Social Services have not shared important information.

But this head teacher's comment reflects the variety of practice which exists:

I have recently moved from one authority to another. Both schools manage social and economic problems and both are in constant dialogue with Social Services. But I have been impressed with the organisation in my new authority, where there is real communication and sharing of information and far more effective practice.

There were a number of observations on teachers' experiences of case conferences, which reflected their concern that poor organisation of some conferences adversely influenced their effectiveness. The ones quoted here are typical of those received:

Many of the ones I have attended have been chaired by persons totally new to the case – this wastes an awful lot of time. I sometimes think procedures get in the way of useful discussion.

The last conference I attended recently was extremely badly managed and created a hostile, confrontational atmosphere. The past history had not been fully explored and evidence gathered from primary school files and staff was being dismissed. Had I not attended, a serious misjudgement would have been made.

Another point which was frequently made emphasised the importance of individuals and the way teachers are viewed by the other professions involved:

If you have a social worker interested and keen to work with a school it makes all the difference to the information which we receive and the way we are listened to.

I think we are sometimes seen as not quite up to the task of commenting on what is best for the child, but of all the professionals present we have had the most contact with, and developed the best understanding of, that child.

Forty per cent of respondents said that there could be difficulties meeting parents at case conferences. Some schools thought that it was inappropriate and unfair for teachers to have to face hostile parents, particularly if Social Services did not appear to appreciate the difficult position of teachers; others felt that their attendance at these conferences jeopardised their future relationship with parents:

On some occasions I felt dragooned by the chair – especially at my early ones. It was difficult to speak absolutely openly in front of parents but I feel confident enough to ask for a confidential slot now.

This point was also reflected in the following comment:

Sometimes I feel that conferences are ineffective in providing adequately for children's welfare, because participants are not always able to be frank.

The majority of respondents (54%) would welcome additional training which would enable them to fulfil their role in case conferences more effectively. A few referred to relevant training which they had received and which had helped them to approach conferences more confidently. The training which was sought by most schools was, in fact, quite basic:

It would be helpful if Social Services would explain the procedures and indicate when it is appropriate for school representatives to speak.

We have repeatedly asked for a training video to be made to introduce staff to case conferences – so far without success.

It is particularly important to train class teachers who, sometimes, should be present at case conferences.

It has long been recognised that one of the reasons why schools are sometimes not represented at case conferences is that it is not always possible to provide cover for the relevant teacher in the school. Most schools (65%) claimed to have difficulties funding supply cover for case conferences, although 47% were able to provide cover from within the school, however difficult. A few schools referred to their LEAs meeting the cost of supply cover from their contingency funds. In many primary schools the head teacher attended conferences as supply cover was then not needed, but this still left other schools facing real problems:

We feel we should be represented and that it is important to attend so we find the funds (or the means) although our budget is very tight.

We will cover from school staff but this is extremely difficult at times and puts extra demands on others.

The disproportionate number of case conferences which schools in certain areas have to attend causes a heavy and unfair demand on already inadequate budgets. The approximate cost of a head teacher attending a conference is £90-£100. If another teacher attends it goes well above that figure. Then there is the cost of the teacher and clerical time in preparing a report. And this is for every conference we attend and we attend over ten each year.

Ability of teachers to recognise abuse and child protection training

While the respondents were reasonably confident that they would be able to recognise signs of abuse in children in their care and act on them, most (88%) were concerned that this would not be the case for all teachers. In fact one third of all respondents were extremely concerned that abuse could go unnoticed because of teachers' inexperience and lack of training.

While the majority of schools thought that the organisation of this training should be the responsibility of their LEAs, they wanted Social Services Departments to be involved at every stage in the training process and to be available to give schools the benefit of their support. The solution was seen to lie in the provision of good quality, multi-agency training available for all staff, and not just for the designated teacher, as a way of drawing on relevant expertise and allowing the participants time to discuss how each service approached the definition of abuse.

It was also evident that some schools had received a great deal of help from other agencies. In particular, a number of them appreciated the help that they had received from school doctors and nurses over specific cases and saw the potential advantages of establishing closer working relationships. However, in many areas the contact which health professionals have with schools has been cut back considerably and there was some apprehension about the effects this would have on schools' confidence in dealing with abuse. Where teachers had benefited from such support they were anxious to harness this expertise by involving doctors and nurses in training sessions.

The accompanying comments contained many references to 'good' training which had been provided by LEAs, Social Services and other agencies. It is evident that initiatives aimed at training designated teachers had made a considerable contribution to the level of awareness of child protection issues in schools and that other members of staff had been involved in training programmes both within schools and at LEA and ACPC level. There were, however, replies that clearly reflected issues with which schools are having to grapple.

There were those which referred to the need to improve the level of knowledge of newly qualified teachers (NQTs), both during their training period and during their initial years in schools. A number of them, who were involved in training and supporting NQTs, would clearly welcome advice and guidance on how to approach this. There are pressures on schools to maintain child protection training for staff (teaching and non-teaching) especially with a regular turnover of staff where a level of prior knowledge could not be assumed and there is an imperative to update and remind all staff about child protection policies, procedures and indicators of abuse. While it was evident that many schools attempted this, some replies referred to this being little more than a theoretical exercise if staff did not have relevant experience. On a very practical note there was a plea by some for a regular reminder to be sent to schools to conduct these updates as they could be overlooked when other training needs were identified.

A few respondents believed that child protection training was best done in schools and conducted by their own staff in order to stress the school's perspective. Far more wanted to see training provided by other professionals involved in the child protection process in order to alert staff to the role of the school in the spectrum of events and draw on a variety of experiences, rather than concentrate on the narrower perspective of head teachers and other responsible teachers. However there was some concern expressed about trainers who themselves had had limited experience of teaching who were given the responsibility to then train teachers and a number of experienced designated teachers believed that their expertise could be appropriately harnessed, especially within a multi-agency approach.

While there was a widespread recognition of the importance of this training not all schools were able to do all that they wished because of the increasing pressures on curriculum time, further government directives about what should be taught and how, with the attendant training that this necessitated, and the other demands which are made on limited budgets.

Vulnerability of teachers who report abuse

Eighty-seven per cent of schools in the study had some concern about teachers' own vulnerability when they report abuse, with more than half of these indicating a reasonably high level of concern. Most respondents thought some form of additional support was needed about how best to deal with this sensitive area, with schools, LEAs and Social Services being seen as having a key role in working together over this. Other agencies were also mentioned by about 10% of schools as sources of potential help, the most popular of these being the Police, NSPCC and the Education Welfare Service.

Most of those who chose to make any additional comments expressed concerns about the potential repercussions for teachers and others involved in making a child protection referral, some of whom highlighted the particular problems which faced staff who lived in the same community as parents. There were many calls for effective support to be given in these circumstances and for it to be incorporated into school and LEA policies and procedures, which would recognise that support and even protection might be necessary and give a commitment to providing this.

Many schools do include an explanation of their role in relation to child protection in material given to parents and this was identified by some as playing a useful part in setting out their responsibility to act. Similarly, schools found it helpful if Social Services, when following up a referral, explained that schools had no choice but to follow procedures that are in the best interests of the child. Some replies described measures taken by schools and Social Services which were designed to support and protect teachers and which were viewed very positively. These included assurances that no teacher would ever be named or otherwise identified and the provision of professional counselling for staff involved in child protection cases. However, there were instances where Social Services had failed to give this support, such as in this case:

A referral often destroys the relationship with a family at a time when it is most needed. We have had problems when Social Services have named individual teachers and passed on information which we had stressed had been given in confidence.

But the main concern expressed by respondents was the importance of recognising this vulnerability at a time when, in the light of what they perceived to be the increasing level of violence by parents in schools:

We all know — and I think it is widely accepted — that teachers are more vulnerable than ever before.

A recent referral, which was subsequently managed badly, left two designated teachers at physical risk of attack from parents.

Uncertainties about contacting Social Services

Just under two-thirds of schools reported some degree of uncertainty about when to contact Social Services in relation to a child protection concern, and for half of these it was quite a major problem. The biggest source of potential support in reducing the level of apprehension was seen to be by improving the channels of communication with Social Services, but LEAs and schools were also seen to have an important role in this process. A small number of schools suggested other areas of support, notably from the Education Welfare Service and NSPCC.

A small number of schools had no experience of direct contact with Social Services as all referrals were made through the Education Welfare Service, but this was not the most usual route. Some respondents commented on how helpful Social Services were when they contacted them to discuss a child protection issue. A few areas operated a helpline or support service whereby schools were able to discuss concerns before making a full referral and those that had access to such support were very appreciative of it. Many others wanted such a service and argued strongly for its introduction in more areas. While it was clear from the results summarised above that schools see Social Services as the major potential source of support, many respondents commented on why, from the perspective of the school, relationships and communication between the two agencies were not always effective.

As far as many schools were concerned the main concerns about their current contacts with Social Service focused on four main areas:

■ The perception that the response from Social Services was not always consistent:

I have reported very similar cases and had diametrically opposed responses. It could be because one child is already known, but I suspect it was just different judgement. It is very difficult to deal with, whatever the reason.

■ The response from Social Services was not always within the timescale seen as desirable by schools where staff may want a response before the end of the school day when children will be expected home by parents.

■ The difficulties which have been experienced in getting Social Services to respond to concerns around neglect and emotional abuse.

■ The worries which were engendered when referrals were not thought to have been acted upon or considered not to have been taken sufficiently seriously:

Part of the problem is the level of evidence required for another agency to take over your concerns. A child may be presenting a great difficulty but across the borough it may not be seen to be significant. How can these two levels of evidence ever be rationalised?

At the same time as identifying their concerns possible solutions were suggested. As well as the provision of a system for informal discussion of concerns described above, the extension of multi-agency training and the development of closer personal links between the different agencies would improve knowledge of each other's work, extend their expertise and deepen trust in each other's ability to make professional judgements:

The LEA has a crucial role in liaison between Education and Social Services. Many cases are not clear-cut and their satisfactory resolution depends on trusted, sound working relationships between key professionals.

In my view it is important that the school staff know and trust local social workers responsible for child protection. All too often staff turnover and frequent internal re-organisation in our local Social Services office preclude this.

However, both where good relationships existed and where improvements were needed, the future was seen to be increasingly uncertain, because budget cuts were leading to reduced staffing levels and fewer resources to support families.

The possibility of some teachers attempting to handle a situation without passing on information

Schools were asked to say if they had any concerns about the possibility of teachers trying to handle child protection issues on their own without reference to the procedures in place or the appropriate colleague. Although over half of respondents (55%) thought that it could happen, most did not regard it as a major concern and believed that once teachers identified a concern they would pass it on to the designated teacher.

Further training in the area of child protection for all teachers has already emerged as an area where additional effort is required and this was reflected in the comments which were made in relation to the possibility of teachers acting on their own. While the majority were confident that teachers were aware of the policies which were in place and that they were reminded of these at regular intervals in training sessions and/or by internal circulars, there were those who expressed some disquiet about the lack of awareness on child protection procedures which some newly qualified and other inexperienced teachers may have.

Communication between different agencies

Eighty-four per cent of schools expressed some level of concern about the way the different agencies involved in the child protection process communicated with each other, with two-thirds of these being very concerned. For the most part it was their channels of communication with Social Services that drew comment. Again most schools thought that this could only be improved by the schools themselves and Social Services Departments taking direct action, although many did see a co-ordinating role for LEAs. A small proportion of schools did indicate other agencies with whom they would like to see improved communication, notably health agencies (particularly general practitioners (GPs), the Police and the Education Welfare Service.

Some schools were clearly satisfied with the way the various agencies involved communicated with each other, but significantly more comments reflected a range of dissatisfactions with the process, mainly focusing on the failure of Social Services to keep them up-to-date with the progress of cases and with the frequent absence of information or any involvement on the part of GPs and other medical services. However, alongside came an acknowledgement by some that the pressure of work and time constraints which operated in all the relevant professions militated against efficient communication and that this could only be addressed by additional resources and possibly even legislation.

There was, however, one group of children that concerned a large number of respondents and these were those suspected of suffering neglect. While it was not always judged to be appropriate to make a child protection referral because previous attempts had not led to any action being taken, schools were very reluctant to do nothing. This teacher was far from alone in expressing these sentiments:

There seems to be a large gap in provision for children, though not necessarily physically or sexually abused, at risk because their parent(s) has/have abdicated responsibility or lost control. They are effectively suffering from the consequences of neglect but Social Services appear not to have the resources to pick up these cases or to follow up our concerns. There needs to be more provision for family support. Education Welfare is sometimes able to fill the gap but only when they go beyond their remit in this LEA. They certainly do not have the resources required. For all the talk of multi-agency work, in my experience there is little or no contact between Child Mental Health Services and schools and similarly between GPs and schools.

How best to support/deal with children

Eighty-eight per cent of schools reported having some concerns about how they could best support children who disclose abuse to staff, with well over half saying that it was something which caused considerable concern. The most frequently mentioned potential source of support was seen to be Social Services, although a substantial proportion also mentioned the role of LEAs in working with schools to establish mechanisms which would not interfere with any inquiry which was initiated. Some schools also mentioned health professionals, NSPCC and the Education Welfare Service as possible partners in attempting to provide better support for children than was currently available.

Alongside went comments which focused on the difficulties which schools faced in knowing how best to support children in the period around the disclosure. A small number of respondents wanted training in counselling skills while far more wanted to see well-resourced counselling services in place, especially as many did not think sufficient time could be found in an already crowded school day.

Support for children subsequent to disclosing abuse

Overall, 90% of the schools were concerned about how best to support children subsequent to disclosing abuse. Again, for over half, it was something which was causing a fairly high level of disquiet and, in an ideal situation, the majority would like to work closely with Social Services and their LEAs to reach a solution. Where other agencies were mentioned they were Health, NSPCC, counselling services and the Education Welfare Service.

Many of the comments from schools referred to the difficulties in knowing how best to support students during the months which followed a disclosure, especially when the official procedures sometimes took a long time to reach completion and where schools were not informed of any treatment programmes which their students were attending. The schools that felt most comfortable about their procedures were those which had received support, training or information from Social Services Departments or where students had access to counselling services. But concerns were also present for pupils who have alleged abuse that is not subsequently proven:

Without evidence nothing can happen. There should be the opportunity to talk to someone for a period of time. If abuse has not been proven it does not mean it is not happening.

Or where the abuse had occurred some time before but where the pain remained:

We have many traumatised children in this school. As a staff we work together to try to build up their trust in us and to make school a safe place for them to be. But we do not have the skills to help them understand their experiences or to make sense of what has happened to them. The shame is that no one else seems to be doing it either.

Support for teachers who deal with abuse

The majority of schools (82%) were concerned about how best to support teachers who are faced with dealing with children who may have experienced abuse, with half viewing it as a major issue. Most schools thought they needed additional counselling or advice either from within the school or their LEAs, although many also thought that Social Services could also be involved. Only a small proportion of schools or LEAs already provided some sort of support for teachers involved in child protection cases, and far more schools felt that the pressures under which some teachers operate in such situations needs to be reflected in a system of appropriate support and counselling:

For designated teachers this [counselling] is essential – it can be very stressful, especially for those of us working in 'high risk' areas.

There is not enough time or even expertise to debrief staff after cases have arisen – staff always feel a responsibility and blame themselves for not spotting signs earlier.

It would be good to have some kind of counselling service particularly for those teachers who deal with very serious abuse cases. I think we often forget that social workers have regular supervision which is not available to teachers.

The handling of accusations made by pupils against teachers

Most schools (79%) said they were concerned about how to handle accusations made by pupils against teachers; the majority indicated that these concerns were not only of a reasonably high level, but that they had increased in recent years as some high profile cases had attracted media attention. While most realised the importance of referring to, and following, their own policies if an accusation was made, once again schools mainly looked to LEAs, and to a lesser extent Social Services, for advice and support. Only 6% mentioned any other agencies, although these schools clearly identified the Police, Trade Unions and Professional Associations as possible sources of support.

The additional comments reflected the fact that fortunately most schools have not had to deal with such a situation, although it did not stop many of them feeling either apprehensive about the possibility or unsure of what would then be the appropriate procedures. While some LEA and school policies clearly covered this contingency, others either did not or respondents were unaware of them. Some respondents expressed additional concerns about the time which such investigations could take and, whilst acknowledging the importance of ensuring every pupil's safety and well-being, the vulnerability of teachers to such accusations.

Relationships with parents involved in child protection cases

Ninety-two per cent of schools said they had some concerns about how to maintain relationships with parents when the schools were involved in child protection cases and two-thirds of respondents were very concerned about this. Again Social Services and LEAs were identified as the main source of potential support, but the Education Welfare Service, health agencies, NSPCC and the Police were all seen by some schools to have a role to play, particularly in working in partnership with schools to offer appropriate support to parents.

Amongst the comments which accompanied these responses were those which focused on the fear felt by some schools that once they had made a child protection referral based on a concern arising in the home, the relationship with parents would be severely damaged and would either take a long time to be restored or would be beyond repair. There were schools which did not know what the correct response should be and how they should act but there were others which said they made a great deal of effort to work with such parents before and after case conferences, some of whom said they had learnt from watching social workers deal with sensitive, complex situations. One head teacher summarised her approach in the following way:

Relationships can be very sensitive and need to be handled with care. However, an openness of opinion which demonstrates how you care for the child is often the best way forward.

However, not all schools were able to learn from Social Services:

I have found it disturbing at times to be asked by some social workers to speak to parents myself, regarding a direct request for help from a pupil, before they will get involved. My training led me to believe that I should report and then leave the rest to the experts. At these times I have felt very vulnerable and afraid of doing more harm than good.

Related to this were the concerns expressed by teachers in a few secondary schools where major child protection concerns were picked up in the early weeks after children started school and they speculated about the possible reluctance of some primary schools to make referrals and risk relationships with parents. As one teacher put it:

I do worry about the reaction of our feeder primary schools where there seems to be a marked reluctance to make a referral when intelligent, vocal and persuasive parents are involved.

Lack of time to get to know pupils

Just over 70% of schools were concerned about the pressures on their time which inhibited their ability to get to know pupils and for half of these it was proving to be an increasing problem. Very few schools thought any other agency was capable of helping them with this aspect of their work, although the additional comments suggested that schools did not think it was a situation which would improve in the immediate future. Larger classes, a more prescriptive curriculum, reduced staffing levels and the absence of any significant non-teaching time in primary schools were all seen to interfere with teachers' ability to get to know their pupils, but the welfare of children and students in their care was still an obvious priority:

If as a society we really have concerns about the well-being of children, the school is in the vanguard. Teachers sometimes spend more time with children than anyone else, including parents, and usually know more about them than any other agency. There should be resources and staffing provided to allow us to assist and take part properly, without trying to stretch the proverbial bit of string to infinity.

While only a few comments emphasised the primary role of the school as being to teach and how this was being diluted by more time having to be spent on concerns about their students' welfare, far more teachers expressed their commitment to this work but were concerned about how best to balance the increasing pressures from both aspects. In particular, children with emotional and behavioural difficulties were seen to miss out most as mainstream teachers were being expected to meet their needs with inadequate provision and without appropriate training.

Time taken up dealing with child protection issues

A very similar percentage of schools was also concerned about the time taken dealing with child protection issues and about the lack of time available to get to know pupils. Three-quarters of schools expressed such concerns, and for most of them these were about the pressures on certain members of staff. Most respondents looked to the LEA and Social Services for some support over this, but were uncertain what form this could take without additional resources.

Most of the additional comments clearly came from schools where child protection concerns took up an increasing amount of time. One school calculated that child protection related work accounted for 10% of their administrative time. While it was evident that such work was seen to be a priority the amount of time taken up by report-writing, attending case conferences and contacting Social Services not only placed a strain on staff but also on school budgets and sometimes on other students when their usual teachers were not available. A few schools wondered how to address the problem when the responsibility was seen to lie with experienced, senior members of staff even though they were often the ones under most pressure. Although this teacher now worked in a school where there were fewer child protection concerns, her previous experience had not faded from memory:

In my previous school I actually kept a record of time I spent on child protection issues. It dominated my life and when put to OFSTED amazed them! Even Social Services were concerned and took issue with the LEA's personnel section.

Another teacher felt that this work was very rarely acknowledged and that there had been a failure to recognise the full implications if schools could not meet the needs of such children:

Central Government must be made to realise that this area is demanding of time. The abused/disturbed child must be dealt with sympathetically. Until their personal needs are met 'school improvement' cannot take place.

Most respondents thought that the chances of all schools receiving additional resources to help them meet their responsibilities was very remote but a number of them, such as the teachers quoted below, suggested some form of targeted funding:

Schools in areas such as this with particularly high numbers of children on the Child Protection Register and in contact with Social Services ought to receive per capita funding in their budgets, as we do with pupils with special educational needs.

At one stage we had 35 children, 10% of our school population, on the Register. Some schools have never dealt with one child protection concern. This takes time! Children need support.

Other concerns

About one-third of respondents mentioned other areas of concern. These centred on the following areas:

■ the concentration of expertise in the hands of a designated teacher – when absent, schools may be left without specific expertise

■ the time involved in dealing with cases and in getting cases to court

■ the failure of some Social Services Departments to recognise the work done by schools to support children

■ lack of consistency in reporting/recording procedures

■ lack of resources available to Social Services to engage in preventative work

- children being removed from the Child Protection Register without all the issues having been addressed

- difficulties which schools and other agencies seem to have in dealing appropriately with emotional abuse and neglect

- an inconsistent and patchy response to tracing and tracking families, particularly where schools had admitted children and had found out later that a Social Services Department in another part of the country had been working with the family but the local Social Services were unaware of concerns.

Training of staff and others involved in schools

The overwhelming majority of designated teachers with responsibility for child protection (92%) have received appropriate training. Most designated teachers had been on more than one course and were generally positive about them, especially when higher level training had enabled them to train side-by-side with other professionals involved in the child protection process.

Two-thirds of schools replied that other members of staff had received training, most of which had been school based, although there were examples of whole staff training by LEAs and multi-agency led training of school staff. Just over a fifth of schools (22%) said one or more members of their governing bodies had received training, most of which had been provided by LEAs specifically for governors, although there were examples of other models of training provided by Social Services, education welfare officers and others. Some respondents indicated that their governors with responsibility for child protection issues would not require additional training as they were or had been professionally involved in the area, for example as teachers, social workers and lawyers.

The Education Act 1993 made provision for Grants for Education Support and Training (GEST) and, until 1998/1999 when this was replaced by The Standard Fund linked to raising standards and achieving improvement in schools, LEAs were invited to apply for grant support for training under a named area in the annual programme. The GEST programme supported child protection training for two years and enabled many LEAs to offer specialist and general training programmes. Just under half of the responding schools knew that some training had been supported by GEST funding.

Posts to be targeted for training

There was a very strong feeling that training should be directed to all teachers. Responses to this questionnaire indicated that in only two-fifths of schools had teachers, other than the designated teachers, received training (see previous heading) and it was evident that schools wanted all teachers to be receive regular training in recognising the signs of abuse in children as well as in how to respond to suspicions and disclosures. Alongside this were calls for particular attention to be paid to students on teaching practice placements and newly qualified teachers within structured induction programmes. In addition there were repeated references to the need for this training to be available to all other staff and volunteers working in schools, as well as to governors. More specifically, some respondents wanted more detailed training to be available for staff with pastoral responsibilities.

Specific areas where training is needed

In addition to the identified need for ongoing training of all teachers, there was some agreement in the replies about the areas where additional training would be most valuable. These were:

- multi-agency training aimed at increasing the level of understanding of the respective roles of the professionals involved in child protection work

- child abuse issues in the early years

- child on child abuse

- accusations against members of the teaching profession

- identification and action when emotional abuse, neglect or 'failure to thrive' is suspected.

Someone with whom a possible referral could be discussed

Ninety per cent of respondents claimed to have at least one person with whom they could discuss a possible referral. Nine per cent had no one and they all would welcome such a person, and the remaining 1% claimed not to need such support.

The most frequently mentioned source of support was a social worker from the local Social Services team (43%); 25% mentioned an education welfare officer; 23% mentioned other colleagues; 18% referred to a member of the LEA staff and 6% identified the school nurse. (The figures add up to more than 100 as some schools named more than one person to whom they would turn.) There were, of course, other individuals and agencies mentioned and these included other health professionals and members of governing bodies, particularly those with relevant professional expertise.

More help and information

Sixty-five per cent of responding schools would welcome more help and information on child protection issues. They were asked to indicate if they would welcome this from named agencies and their replies are summarised below:

Table 2 Agencies which schools are looking to for support

Named Agency	Percentage of all responding schools
Social Services	50%
Local Education Authorities	47%
Area Child Protection Committees	46%
NSPCC	43%
Trade Union / Professional Association	17%
Other agency	5%

Discussion

Most schools have designated teachers who have received some training, and they have policies in place. A study in the USA (Abrahams, Casey and Daro, 1992) of 568 teachers showed that although the majority of teachers encountered child abuse amongst their students, they did not consider that they had received sufficient training to deal with the problem. In this country over recent years the amount of training available to teachers on child protection has increased, in response to a clarification of their responsibilities. Much of this training has, however, been targeted at designated teachers only. In some authorities and in some schools there have been sessions designed for classroom and subject teachers, as well as for other members of the school community. But such training is neither compulsory nor very widespread. There is reason to be concerned about provision on initial teacher training courses (see Chapter 4) and the recent requirements from the Teacher Training Agency will do little to improve the situation. The responses from schools clearly indicate that there are concerns about how best they should deal with their role in the child protection process. There was little sign of any reluctance to accept the responsibilities of this role but it was clear that many were looking for additional support and training. The challenge will be how to do this.

In Campbell and Wigglesworth's (1993) study 40% of teachers were neither confident of recognising the signs of abuse nor of responding appropriately if approached by a child with signs of abuse. The knowledge of classroom teachers was not as good as that of head teachers in the study, and while the authors acknowledged that extensive training could not be made available to all teachers they believed all teachers needed appropriate skills to respond to children who may be abused. Their response was to advocate greater emphasis on a multi-disciplinary approach to child protection and the roles of other professionals. It was recommended that teachers needed not only to receive information about child abuse but more importantly they needed help in identifying their strength in this area, practical advice on handling disclosures in the school setting and in working effectively with staff from other agencies.

Kirkland, Field and Hazel (1996) also indicate that the main problem under the current *Working Together* guidelines (Home Office et al, 1991) is that knowledge of child protection procedures and an awareness of the issues have not reached all the staff in schools, which is reflected in the responses to this survey. And to reiterate their conclusion, staff turnover and the need then to update and provide a rolling programme of training at a time when resources for all training are under considerable pressure, probably means that in many schools abused children are not always being identified and dealt with in a manner which is consistent with the law and locally agreed procedures.

It was evident from the responses that communication between schools and other agencies, chiefly Social Services, did not always run smoothly. This is not a new discovery and has been identified in a number of inquiries and reports on both sides of the Atlantic (Birchall and Hallett (1995); Zellman (1990). Also in the USA, Tite (1993) looked at teachers' definitions of abuse and examined the relationship between definitions and intervention and she concluded that teachers and the child protection services were not using the same definition. This meant that only 25% of teachers' concerns would be taken seriously by these services. In this country successful referrals rely on teachers and others involved in education understanding the definitions of 'significant harm' and 'at risk' being used by their local Social Services Department, but they also revolve around meeting the criteria which will trigger the threshold for action by the Social Services. It is very probable that many potential referrals are not made because teachers judge, on the basis of past experience, that they would not be acted upon.

Circular 10/95 (Department for Education and Employment, 1995) makes clear that where any abuse is suspected or a sustainable allegation is made teachers and other members of the schools staff should report the information to the designated teacher, who should refer these cases to or discuss them with the investigative agencies according to the procedures established by the local ACPC and, in the case of LEA-maintained schools, the LEA. If a designated teacher is unsure about whether a case should be referred or has a general concern about a child's health or development, he or she can seek advice and support from the local Social Services Department, NSPCC or, in the case of LEA-maintained schools, the LEA's child protection co-ordinator. A child who is not being abused or at risk of abuse may be 'in need' of local authority services, as defined by the Children Act (Section 17) and such cases need to be made known to the Social Services Departments. All this depends on a clear understanding of the aims and objectives of all the agencies involved in the system. One obvious way of achieving this is through multi-agency training that goes beyond a superficial description of procedures. Wattam (1992) and others have written about the complexities that surround the decision to act on individual referrals, but for many teachers the process remains a mystery. Perhaps even more alarming was Jackson's (1994) observation that in ACPCs educational representatives were the least knowledgeable and that the relationship between education and all other agencies was the weakest of all. Professor Jackson went on to comment that while National Curriculum training was compulsory, child protection training was not.

As the data for this report was being collected Sinclair's (1998) research unearthed a very obvious impediment to effective dialogue between schools and Social Services. She found a disturbing lack of knowledge and understanding among Social Services Department staff about the educational system and a similar lack of knowledge amongst teachers of the work of social workers. There is evidence that effective multi-disciplinary work is possible, but that it frequently depends on good inter-personal relationships. Some respondents commented on the benefits that resulted from such liaisons, while others expressed the need for a named individual or support service for sounding out concerns or making referrals. Legislation which demands that professionals must work together for the welfare of the child has long been on the statute book, but the fact that there is still a high level of concern and uncertainty means that a fresh approach and a renewed commitment is required. Sinclair (1994) believes:

There is evidence of a growing tension between professionals in education and Social Services Departments, often despite feelings of goodwill and shared aims, but the ability to work together effectively is being hampered by arguments over budgets and the growing practice of having to contract or buy services once freely exchanged.

In addition, the revised Working Together guidelines are refocused towards children and families in need and away from individual abuse. It is far from clear how services will get the right balance between child protection and family support. Anecdotal evidence from schools indicates even higher levels of concern about their referrals to Social Services failing to trigger what, in their eyes, would be seen as an appropriate response. Given the complexities of such relationships and their importance to the welfare of our children it is imperative that a clear strategy is worked out. At the present time there is an obvious discrepancy between policy and practice. Fundamental to such a strategy which must encompass all agencies and their constituents is a clear, efficient referral system and an identification of training needs, effective communication and appropriate provision. Alongside this it may be time to reconsider the role of the educational social worker. At the present time much of their time is spent working with schools to ensure attendance targets are met. As valuable as this work is it is clear that schools would welcome closer links with Social Services and the time may be right to examine in more detail models from around the world which link the two more closely together.

4 The role of LEAs in child protection

Background

The Department of Education and Science circular on child protection which appeared in 1988 (DES Circular 4/88) attempted to raise the profile of schools within the child protection process. It recommended the procedures which should be in place including the designation of a senior member of the LEA's staff to act as the child protection co-ordinator, the designation of a member of staff within each school as their child protection co-ordinator and the statement that LEA and ACPC procedures should be followed in all circumstances by everyone within the Education Service. Not only was this not statutory, but it appeared at the very time when the role of LEAs was being questioned at many levels, including governmental. Grant maintained status was being introduced, which meant state funded schools were able to leave the orbit of their LEA and be answerable to the Department, and those that chose to stay were given considerable autonomy over their budgets and general management. No longer could LEA priorities be assumed to be school priorities. At the same time the National Curriculum was being introduced with the attendant pressures on schools and LEA advisory teams. It was hardly an auspicious start for an initiative designed to improve the welfare of children. LEAs were clearly more active in this area but there had been little research to indicate exactly how they were working or how they viewed their involvement.

The survey

A telephone call was made to every LEA to determine the name of the person with responsibility for child protection in that authority. A questionnaire was then sent to that person in September 1997. In 26% of authorities this was the Deputy Director or Assistant Director of Education and in 25% it was the Chief or Principal Education Welfare Officer. In other areas it was a Senior Education Officer or Education Officer (10%), a Manager of Pupil Services (8%) or a variety of other posts, details of which are included in Appendix A. Not all questionnaires were completed by this person, although in those authorities where the Chief/Principal Education Social Work/Welfare Officer was the responsible individual they did do so. Assistant Directors of Education were far more likely to have passed it to those with day-to-day responsibility for child protection issues, such as Education Officers, Education Social Work/Welfare Officers, Managers of Pupil Services and Child Protection Workers where such departments had been established.

A total of 154 questionnaires was distributed: questionnaires were sent to the new Unitary authorities including those which were to come into existence in April 1998 and replies were received from 85% of LEAs/Unitary Authorities which were canvassed. The questionnaire covered their current involvement in this area, the types of schools with which they worked, how this was funded and their views on how this work would develop.

LEA guidance on child protection

The majority of authorities (98% of respondents) replied that they did provide written guidance of some sort to schools, although only 56% of authorities claimed to have drawn up a specific document for education, with most of the others distributing ACPC procedures to schools and a few sending schools information circulars which had been prepared for training courses. All the authorities were represented on their ACPCs and the guidance prepared for schools were all to follow the principles of ACPC Guidelines. In nearly every case the person with responsibility for child protection also represented the authority on the ACPC, but 25% of LEAs had more than one representative, reflecting the fact that these senior members of staff were then joined by colleagues who had more day-to-day responsibility for child protection. In 80% of LEAs schools were represented on ACPCs or on their subgroups. But this means that in one fifth of LEAs schools do not have such representation. Further research is clearly needed to investigate the reasons for this, as well as the mechanisms which those individuals who do represent schools use to link with their constituencies. A number of comments from LEA officials indicated that there were often difficulties in recruiting teachers to these groups, as they represented yet one more commitment on top of many other responsibilities. Even where there is representation one individual may 'represent' a large number of schools spread over a wide geographical area and it would often be difficult, if not impossible, to arrange feedback at an appropriate forum.

LEAs, child protection and grant maintained and independent schools

LEAs clearly have a statutory responsibility for their own schools but not for any of the schools that chose to become grant maintained. Similarly, LEAs have no statutory responsibility at all for schools in the independent sector. But it was known that some LEAs were working with schools in both these sectors, although the extent of these links had been unclear.

Seventy per cent of responding LEAs had grant maintained schools within their boundaries and, perhaps surprisingly, the majority (80% of these LEAs) considered they had some responsibility towards them in relation to child protection issues. This would certainly be nothing more than a 'moral' responsibility, and in many cases the schools themselves had looked to their former authorities to support them in an area where they may have felt their new-found independence left them feeling too vulnerable or exposed. A higher proportion of LEAs had local independent schools (94%) and, perhaps even more surprisingly, just over half considered that they had some responsibility towards these schools.

Grant maintained schools

■ *Documentation:* 77% provided relevant documentation to grant maintained schools at the same time as it went to their own schools and a further 9% would do so if requested.

■ *Training:* 49% extended their training on child protection to grant maintained schools and a further 32% would be willing to respond to any request for training made from that sector (almost all of which would be charged).

■ *Referral reporting route:* 53% would make child protection referrals for grant maintained schools and a further 32% would be willing to consider doing so, but most respondents also said that they would prefer schools to liaise directly with Social Services Departments, as the vast majority of LEA schools already do.

■ *Advice:* 59% of LEAs with grant maintained schools said they would always give these schools advice on child protection issues and another 26% would consider doing so in relation to a specific request.

Independent schools

■ Documentation: 47% provided relevant documentation to independent schools at the same time as it went to their own schools and a further 18% would do so if requested.

■ *Training:* 14% extended their training on child protection to independent schools and a further 44% would be willing to respond to any request for training made from that sector (and two LEAs had produced a training pack for independent schools). Independent schools may receive training and other information through the ACPC multi-agency training group.

■ *Referral reporting route:* 24% would make child protection referrals for independent schools and a further 19% would be willing to consider doing so, but again most respondents also said that they would prefer schools to liaise directly with Social Services Departments.

■ *Advice:* 27% of LEAs with independent schools in their areas said they would always give these schools advice on child protection issues and another 36% would consider doing so in relation to a specific request.

A small proportion of LEAs also offered grant maintained and independent schools a range of other services including crisis support for staff and pupils and background information on child protection for parents.

The responses clearly indicated that LEAs take differing approaches to their relationships with schools other than their own. Some automatically sent out LEA documentation and would respond to any request, while others would either be willing to consider individual requests and others had not considered the issue at all. Fifteen per cent of LEAs said they had offered training and consultation to independent schools on behalf of their ACPCs, but that it had been declined. In most cases non-LEA schools would pay for such training, but there were LEAs continuing to provide the same child protection services to grant maintained schools as they had before the change in status – and without any cost!

A small number of respondents actually expressed uncertainty about their responsibility for these schools, particularly independent schools, and there were certainly LEAs who would be very reluctant to accept any responsibility for grant maintained schools. This LEA officer was not the only one to view grant maintained schools as completely outside their remit:

The purpose of the Government in setting up GM schools was to remove our powers and responsibilities from as many things as possible. Our ACPC procedures specify that Social Services have the responsibility for non-LEA education establishments.

Some questions still remain unanswered. There were LEAs who had no contact with grant maintained and/or independent schools and it was far from clear what support, if any, these schools received from other agencies in relation to child protection procedures or training. Grant maintained status disappeared and all categories of school which have been introduced to take their place have come within their LEA's remit, at least for some purposes, one of which is child protection. But the position of independent schools is clearly an area that demands further research.

Extent of LEAs' responsibilities for child protection

LEAs no longer have the responsibility for checking that their schools have child protection policies and procedures in place, but as it was known that some LEAs still keep an oversight they were asked about this and the results are recorded in Table 3. All LEAs said they offered a consultation service to the schools in their areas and, as indicated above, this would often be available to grant maintained schools and in some cases to independent schools. Eighty-seven per cent of LEAs said they included details about the service in relevant documentation sent to schools. In 80% of LEAs this was provided by the Education Social Work/Welfare Services, although in some cases this was in conjunction with other agencies such as the Education Psychology Service or a specific child protection service or with other LEA staff. In the other LEAs this service was provided entirely by others such as child protection co-ordinators, Children's Services managers and School Support sections.

Ninety per cent of LEAs included training on Child Protection issues as a standard item in their training programme, although a third of authorities made it clear that this was solely or largely provided with Social Services or on a multi-agency basis and many other authorities employed independent trainers who sometimes worked alongside Education or Social Services staff. In addition there were many comments indicating that LEAs would not be able to continue with the current level of training once GEST (Grants for Education Support and Training)[1] ceased.

Table 3 LEAs and involvement with schools in relation to child protection

	LEA Schools	Grant Maintained Schools	Independent Schools
Written policies on child protection	79 %	51%	10 %
Procedures in relation to child protection	89%	57%	20%
Designated teachers with responsibility for child protection	98%	66%	9%
Procedures to communicate policy and procedures to all staff	82%	45%	7%
A nominated governor with responsibility for child protection[2]	60%	14%	1%

■ *Ninety-five per cent provided training for designated teachers,* although this varied from a two hour training session to a few where there were three staged planned programmes (over six or more days) and to a four part course which covered training on their role in case conferences and communication and listening skills.

■ *Seventy per cent provided training for pastoral staff,* but this would usually be a basic awareness course in response to a request from schools although some LEAs also said they would generally expect the designated teachers to provide training and support.

■ *Sixty-five per cent provided training for all teaching staff,* again usually in response to a request from schools or on a rolling programme where a certain percentage of the LEA's schools is covered each year. However, there were many LEAs where staff who had received training were expected to pass this on to their colleagues.

■ *Sixty-four per cent provided training for all school staff,* usually where requested, but a few LEAs had devised a roadshow or other training session, either focusing exclusively on child protection or as part of a 'Keep Safe' initiative.

■ *Fifty-eight per cent provided training for peripatetic staff* and 45% of LEAs extended this training to youth workers, home tutors and others having direct contact with children.

---

[1] Child Protection was a specified area for such DfEE grants in 1995-6 and 1997-8.

[2] A number of LEAs said they had just begun to incorporate in their documentation the suggestion that schools may consider nominating a governor with responsibility for child protection.

■ *In addition 66 per cent of LEAs provided training for school governors*, some being in response to governors' requests for clarification of their responsibilities in relation to any allegations of misconduct by head teachers while others said the emphasis was on policies and procedures.

LEAs were asked to provide details of the proportion of schools located in their areas which had been represented on child protection training during the past three years. Seventy-eight per cent of LEAs were able to provide this information in relation to their own schools. In almost one-third of authorities 90% or more of their schools had been represented. However, in 13% of LEAs 50% or less of primary schools had had a member of staff at any appropriate training. As far as LEA secondary and special schools were concerned the proportions of all schools represented were somewhat higher. In 32% of LEAs all secondary schools had been represented and 45% of special schools. Of concern, however, was the fact that in 19% of LEAs 50% of secondary schools had not attended and in 13% of LEAs this was the case in relation to special schools. Overall 10% of LEAs had had fewer than 25% of their schools represented on training in the past three years. One LEA respondent, from an authority which had had a good proportion of its schools represented on training, hinted at the effort sometimes required to attain this:

We have worked at building up generally good relationships with our schools and to encourage them to come on training but there are a few who do not respond to anything and who make no response no matter how hard we try.

So while LEAs may offer training, individual schools have responsibility for their budgets and for managing their staff and will decide their own priorities.

A number of comments referred to the difficulties faced by schools in sending staff to day time training. In some cases LEAs had been able to pay for supply cover, particularly where GEST money had been available or had increased the number of after-school sessions. But other factors were also at work:

With the introduction of Local Management of Schools and devolved budgets schools are able to prioritise their training needs. Unfortunately child protection has to compete with all the elements of the National Curriculum and when money is scarce the National Curriculum and the drive to raise standards wins.

These figures represent only those schools who have attended training which has been organised or supported by their LEAs. With devolved budgets and greater school autonomy it is possible for schools to buy in training from other providers.

Similar information was requested in relation to grant maintained schools. Nearly three-quarters of all responding LEAs had grant maintained schools within their areas. Nearly half of these did not keep the appropriate records. It is difficult to obtain a clear picture of the level of penetration of training without examining the number of grant maintained schools in each LEA but it was evident from the replies that while many grant maintained schools have been involved in LEA child protection training a significant proportion of grant maintained primary, secondary and special schools have not been, but it is possible that they had bought in independent trainers or used other providers.

Eighty-six of the 130 LEAs had an independent special school in their area, although of these only 28 had any information on how many of these schools had been represented on LEA-based training in the past three years and in most of these (18) none had attended.

In the years 1995/1996 and 1997/1998 LEAs in England were able to apply for grant support on their expenditure to support their work on child protection. In both years this was to enable senior teachers with designated responsibility for child protection to receive appropriate and practical in-service training. Over 90% of LEAs had made at least one bid for GEST funding to support child protection training. At the first round 72% of responding LEAs had done so and 96% of these were successful; at the second round 85% of respondents had bid with a success rate of 94%. Most of the training supported by GEST had been aimed solely at designated teachers. Much of this was designed for those who had not received appropriate training or where such training had taken place some time before, but in a small number of LEAs specific topics were identified for higher level training and these included contributing to case conferences, working within core groups and supporting colleagues in relation to child protection concerns.

Some LEAs had devolved this money to schools and they were not always sure how it had been used; others had done this at the first round and their experience led them to hold it centrally when their second bid was successful to ensure that it was used only on child protection training. The overwhelming majority of authorities which had been successful said that the grant had enabled training to take place which would not otherwise have been possible or had allowed teachers to attend existing training. While there was some uncertainty about how much funding would be available to the ACPCs from the Department of Health, and the hope that some of this would support training of teachers, there was a widespread acceptance that once GEST funding was not available the overall level of training of those working or associated with schools would be severely curtailed. Most LEAs believed that while some training would continue to be provided, GEST funding had enabled many LEAs to develop and expand training in this area and there was considerable concern and pessimism about their ability to sustain this without additional resources. There was a realisation that many schools would be unable to find the money to send teachers on courses and some criticism that an area as important as child protection should depend on intermittent funding subject to bids:

The GEST funding is less than necessary to do a comprehensive job. The uncertain and transitory nature of the funding hinders the maintenance of an appropriate high profile training programme.

Overall, most LEAs envisaged continuing to train designated teachers, but in some cases this would be only for those newly appointed to post and would not extend to any updating or higher level training.

LMS (Local Management of Schools) formulae are the means used for allocating resources to individual schools within their areas. DfEE Circular 10/95 (Department for Education and Employment, 1995) requires LEAs and other bodies with a duty under the Children Act (1989) to ensure that supply cover is provided, if required, when a designated teacher or other member of staff attends a child protection conference (or the designated teacher attends training). But only just over a quarter of LEAs in fact made an allocation for child protection in their LMS formulae specifically designed to enable schools to be represented at case conferences. However, it was widely recognised that even where this allocation was made it usually failed to take account of the demands made on some schools by the increasing number of case conferences and core group and other meetings which they were expected to attend. Only a small number of LEAs specifically referred to an 'additional needs' element to support schools in areas of social deprivation.

Sixty-two per cent of respondents were involved in multi-agency training, but most of these references were to courses run by a multi-agency team for educational personnel, rather than examples of educational personnel being involved in multi-agency courses for other professionals, although there were a few examples of this. Some LEAs were planning to be involved in multi-agency training at a later stage when, and if, they were able to complete the base-line training of their own staff. In other areas even this base-line training had a multi-agency approach, as in this authority:

All statutory agencies are represented on the ACPC training team who train together and provide training for their own agencies and as a team for others. The LEA has two trainers on this team – the Principal Education Welfare Officer and the Advisor for Personal and Social Education. Training is also provided for schools to support children and young people who might be abused.

So while in some authorities multi-agency working appeared to be working well, in others there was the implication that much work still needed to be done to improve liaison and understanding:

As an authority I think we have very good relations with Social Services. The training is very good on child protection – it is very well organised and it is multi-professional. It is well put together, But there will always be a problem between those reporting, who can be very concerned by what is facing them, and those reacting. There is still an element of not understanding the pressures under which each is operating.

I think what has to be stressed is the respect which exists in this LEA for social workers in this area.... But one of the problems is the level of staffing in Social Services. They cannot cope and we know it. We are aware of the problems which they have. As an LEA we should make it even clearer that posts cannot disappear, we need more social workers. At multi-agency meetings Social Services are very much on the defensive. I want them to tell us how badly off they really are and not to take examples as criticism. I think we have to stand up and shout together.

Over 90% of authorities have a procedure in place which requires designated teachers to make referrals directly to Social Services, although in most cases they are then required to notify the responsible officer in the LEA. Other patterns that emerged from the survey were authorities which required schools to make any referral via the Education Social Work Service/Education Welfare Service or to contact the responsible officer in the LEA who then had contact with Social Services. Only one LEA set out all three routes as alternatives with schools choosing the one they wished to use.

Seventy-two per cent have taken some action to reduce the risk of staff being involved in an allegation of abuse. For the most part this took the form of codes of practice, specific documentation, recommendations for relevant inclusions in school policies, and a limited amount of training. Ninety-one per cent of LEAs had recommended procedures to schools for dealing with allegations of abuse against teachers and 84% had made similar recommendations in relation to head teachers. However, there were many comments which indicated that dealing with actual allegations was taking up an increasing amount of time and effort.

The survey was conducted prior to the DfEE statement (DfEE Circular 10/98) on acceptable levels of restraint that could be used by teachers on pupils. At that point 68% had issued guidance for schools on this matter. Many LEAs commented that they would be drafting or redrafting guidance in the light of the definition contained in the Education Act (1997) of 'reasonable force'. In developing these procedures most LEAs had worked with professional associations and teaching unions in the development of the procedures and statements in relation to allegations made against staff; over 60% also commented that all policies and guidance are discussed with these bodies.

The new Unitary Authorities who replied to the survey were using the policies and procedures that they had inherited and were in the process of reviewing how appropriate they were. Since this time some Unitary Authorities have developed a pattern of service provision where all children's services come within the same structure. This was a response to the delineation and consequent failures of communication within a traditional model. The advantages have now been recognised by the Social Services Inspectorate.

The survey of schools clearly indicated that teachers wanted more support in dealing with questions of child protection, and looked to LEAs as an important provider of such help. But overall very few LEAs referred to support or discussion groups. There were only three references to authorities bringing designated teachers together as a group to provide them with the opportunity to talk about their work and to extend their training by giving them the opportunity to make contact and strengthen links with colleagues in other schools.

Discussion

Although LEAs have clearly tried to respond to the demands which have been made of them, particularly over the past decade, the work generated by the responsibility for child protection is growing fast. This had been accelerated since attention had turned to the increasing number of allegations made against school staff. At the same time schools have gained increasing levels of autonomy, the very existence of LEAs has been questioned and there has been a real reduction in staffing levels, both in schools and at authority level. This has resulted in even more pressure on staff and not surprisingly, in a vital area of work that needs to take priority over other immediate demands, a higher level of stress.

Many respondents felt that there were two main aggravating factors. The introduction of delegated budgets has limited the LEAs' powers to monitor the process and the OFSTED inspections of authorities are standards focused which once again fails to highlight the importance of this work. One LEA officer summed up his feelings in the following comment:

It is an aspect, but curriculum attainment is what really matters, not the real factors which may have an effect on attainment.

It is evident that GEST money had supported a great deal of training. It is also clear that many LEAs are trying to sustain an appropriate level of training in their areas. The survey has highlighted some of the positive developments which had happened and some of the difficulties which LEAs were facing. The situation has changed in the interim. Grant maintained status has disappeared and these schools have been brought back into their LEAs. The pressure to meet National Curriculum standards continues, but over the coming period the role of the schools in relation to the welfare and protection of children will be further highlighted as the requirements of the new *Working Together* document become a reality. It is still unclear if any additional support will be made available to LEAs to enable them to give schools the help which they will undoubtedly need to fulfil their responsibilities. It is already time to take a fresh look at what LEAs are doing.

5 Seeing beyond the circulars

The most significant piece of legislation concerning the welfare of children in the UK is the Children Act (1989). The development of state intervention in childhood has been said to reflect the growing recognition of the child as a person with rights, but it would seem far more likely that those who framed the Act were hoping to achieve a better balance between child protection on the one hand and the rights of the family on the other. The Introduction states:

The Act seeks to protect children both from the harm which can arise from failures or abuse within the family and from the harm which can be caused by unwarranted intervention in their family life. There is a tension between those objectives which the Act seeks to regulate so as to optimise the overall protection provided for children in general.

The Children Act (1989) established the welfare of the child as the paramount principle. The Act specifies that local authorities have a general duty to safeguard and promote the welfare of children in need within their area and, so far as is consistent with their duty, to promote the upbringing of such children by their families. It is clear that intervention must positively promote the child's welfare and must be in the child's best interests. But as welcome as the Children Act was it has contributed to the complexity of child protection and to the level of understanding required by professionals whose work impinges on it. Finding that a child has experienced abuse or neglect is not sufficient or even necessary for an entry to be recorded on the Child Protection Register. The number of children recorded on these registers is not the same as the number who will have experienced abuse or neglect (See Corby, 1990). For example, registers contain the names of children who have not been abused or neglected but who are judged to be at risk and they omit the names of children who have been abused or neglected but not seen to need further protection. In order for a child to be placed on a Child Protection Register a Child Protection Conference has to find that to be an essential next step.

But while declaring the welfare of the child to be paramount the State was also taking a step back from intervening in the lives of families. The reasons for this lay in the events of the 1980s. In the mid to late 1980s there were concerns expressed that intervention was occurring too readily and too frequently in the lives of families. There were a number of well-publicised cases where children were removed from their homes. Even though subsequent analyses of these cases serve, for the most part, to justify intervention, the very public criticism by the media of Social Services must have undermined the faith of many in them. So at a time when legislation was being formulated which put children's welfare at the centre there was a very public questioning of the competency of the key agency in the proposed procedures. It is very difficult to measure the damage inflicted on the social work profession by this and other public vilification of individuals at the centre of child abuse tragedies. At a time when teachers' role in relation to child protection was being more clearly defined the possible shortcomings of the agency with which they were expected to work more closely was headline news.

It has already been noted that the Act made it clear that local authorities have a responsibility to children in need of preventative services and placed a duty on them to respond to this need. However, local authorities have continued to give priority to children in need of protection because they have not had the resources to do otherwise. The Audit Commission (Audit Commission, 1994) carried out an inspection of eight local authorities between 1993 and 1995 and found that cases of children in need were seen as having a very low priority unless they met the definition of abuse or neglect. The increasing pressure on the services meant that this category of children tended to receive a lower level of services than their condition demanded. There has continued to be a shortage of services to support children in need who are left at home, even though this has long been recognised as a major shortcoming of the system. Priority was given to children who were seen to need protection and in many cases referrals were made to child protection services to gain access to services. So, although it was the intention of the Act to identify children in need and provide services for them, a large number of families who should have been given support found themselves subject to investigatory procedures. The demand for services overwhelmed many local departments and continues to do so. Having a Child Protection Conference and subsequent entry on a Child Protection Register was seen to be the only way of targeting resources on the child and family. But even then more attention was given to the assessment of risk than to the assessment of need. Sharland et al (1996) found that one year after a referral only one-third of children who had experienced sexual abuse had received any appropriate supportive intervention and most of those that did received only limited support. This has been confirmed by work conducted over the past year (Baginsky et al., 2000).

The responsibility given to schools by the Children Act (1989) and the subsequent guidance represented a move towards recognising the role which many schools had assumed they had for many years. There were certainly teachers who believed they were there solely to teach as well as those who saw official interference as a damaging prospect for families whom they knew and judged to be coping within the limits of their abilities. Echoes of these feelings can still be heard although they have grown a great deal fainter. It is probably safe to assume that most teachers now recognise that they have this responsibility. The survey of schools (reported in Chapter 3) indicates a willingness amongst designated teachers to be involved in this work and a desire to become more effective partners in it. There were, however, many concerns expressed, one of the major ones being how best to improve communication with Social Services Departments.

There are parts of the country where links between Social Services and schools are very good and this usually reflects how much attention has been devoted to making sure it works. There are also individual schools and Social Services teams that have built up excellent working relationships over the years. But the reality is that this is usually not the case. Many schools report having to wait an inordinately long time for Social Services to respond to referrals or being left in the dark about progress. There are still reports from Social Services about the inappropriateness of many referrals from schools. But is that surprising when the author was told by a senior member of the Social Services Department in one of our large cities that schools have never been given any idea of their threshold for action? Surely, if there is any point to a multi-agency approach that should be at the centre of discussions, alongside training on the complexity of decision-making.

This is an important area and its significance was identified in Birchall and Hallett's work (1995). They explored the difficulties involved in arriving at a consensual definition of referral thresholds, leaving some schools confused by Social Services' failure to intervene in cases (or to carry out an initial investigation and decide that further action was not required) where a child protection issue had been identified and reported. This is an area to which Murphy (1995) has also drawn attention. He calls it the 'double bind' present in the British system whereby different definitions of what is serious abuse can lead to child protection referrals from the Education Service not being properly processed or not being made in the first place:

Successful referrals rely, to a large extent, on educational personnel understanding the definition of 'significant harm' which is used by the main processing agency – the Social Services Department.

But on both sides of the Atlantic the focus has subsequently shifted to ways to reduce the demand for services with greater emphasis on screening processes and risk assessments and the development of criteria for response, investigation and follow-up. (See, for example, Waldfogel, 1998). In both countries this has led to attacks on the referral system. There are reports of too many unfounded or unnecessary referrals. There is a tendency to view these as 'false reports' and conclude that there is too much intrusion into family privacy and/or that reporting is a mechanism for gaining control over the poor and socially disenfranchised. The threshold for intervention has consequently risen.

Services have moved not only towards the identification of abuse or neglect, but also the assessment of risk in an attempt to make the most appropriate response. So while a case may pass the threshold for an investigative procedure it may be judged that it should be treated as one where a family support response should be made. This has required greater attention to be paid to the concept of 'child in need'. *Working Together to Safeguard Children* (Department of Health et al, 1999) and the related *Framework for the Assessment of Children in Need and their Families* (Department of Health et al, 2000) recognise the crucial role of the education system and of teachers. In the author's view the shift in emphasis will have limited impact without significant additional resources and a willingness to return to first principles. At least some additional resources may be there. A number of initiatives have been launched with the potential to impact on this area and education, as a partner within a multi-agency approach, plays a key role in all of them. These include Sure Start, the Connexions strategy and social inclusion and pupil support programmes. It now becomes a matter of urgency to make sure that an appropriate response is made and that the initiatives are not nullified by the push to raise standards and achievement in schools at the expense of the long term welfare of all children.

But it is important to view this within a wider context. At the present time there is a chronic shortage of experienced (and even inexperienced) social workers. A variety of reasons (some of which are highlighted in this chapter) have contributed to the haemorrhage of social workers from the statutory services. In some cases the voluntary services have been the beneficiaries but all too often the expertise has been lost altogether. The situation has been aggravated by the many reorganisations which Social Services Departments have experienced. In some of the most deprived and disadvantaged areas often under-resourced services have been judged to fail those they serve, management has been changed, restructuring imposed, and targets raised, along with the stress level of those expected to meet them. New solutions are suggested to meet a growing demand and when the solutions fail to deliver the cycle starts over again.

But organisational change has not only been a feature of Social Services. Health and Education have had their own reorganisations. As far as schools are concerned, at the time when a greater level of co-ordination would have supported the implementation of *Working Together* increasing autonomy was given to schools. Some state schools moved outside the control of the LEAs altogether. Although they have now been brought back under the wing of LEAs it meant that they were not automatically part of the training and support network at a very crucial time. Although it is very unlikely that any LEA would have refused information and support to one of these schools if there was a child protection concern, and some LEAs continued to offer training and much else to these schools, it did make co-ordination and communication more difficult. Even for the majority of schools that stayed with their LEAs, budgets were increasingly devolved to schools and they, in turn, could choose which training to buy into. So even when LEAs provided training it was not always taken up.

Discussions between the author and representatives of local authorities around the country consistently contain reports about poor representation of teachers on multi-agency groups and at training sessions. The responses from schools reported in Chapter 3 indicate that this cannot be because schools do not give a high priority to child protection, but the result of schools deciding on their immediate priorities. At the very time when the schools were officially charged with these additional responsibilities they were having to adapt to the introduction of the National Curriculum and national testing. They have also become subject to very public scrutiny of their test results when they are published in national and local newspapers as league tables. They are regularly inspected by the teams from the Office for Standards in Education (OFSTED). It is certainly not a scenario where pupil welfare will necessarily get the priority it deserves.

We know that child abuse occurs in all classes and cultures, but it does not serve any purpose to ignore the fact that many of the schools finding it difficult to meet the Government's attainment targets contain a higher proportion of students who are seen to be in need or at risk. In some cases a school's definition of these terms is relative. If a child does not have an appropriately warm coat on a winter's day and has not eaten breakfast does this reflect the poverty of the home or does it indicate neglect? It certainly indicates a child in need and action should be taken within the *Working Together* guidelines. But in an area where there are many such needy children how long will it take to get an initial reaction and then to get a co-ordinated response?

It is always easier to identify the problems than to find the solutions. It may be that we need to consider what we actually want to achieve by bringing schools into the equation. The answer has to be one which involves schools in the promotion of children's welfare as equal partners. For this to happen it requires schools to have the appropriate policies, alongside teachers with the necessary training and access to advice to be able to identify children at risk or in need. At the present time, while most designated teachers do receive training its content and frequency differ considerably around the country. For the most part trainee teachers also receive some input on child protection but it is far from consistent across courses. It is time that a planned approach was taken towards this training, both pre-service and in-service.

Student teachers have to meet the standard that requires them to have a working knowledge and understanding of their liabilities and responsibilities in relation to child protection. But there is no guidance on what this should involve. It would be very useful if the DfEE, through the Teacher Training Agency, set out what it expects teachers to know and to be able to do as a result of this training. If this was made clear to courses not only would it serve to raise the profile of child protection, but it would remove some of the uncertainty that sometimes leads to both too little or too much detail being included on some courses. Students have many other priorities during their training period and if anything is to be retained it needs to be presented as crucial information provided in a supportive and appropriate way, with the clear understanding that further training will be provided at a later stage.

On the basis of work conducted for this report and subsequent research it is evident that while most students do see it as an important aspect of their work, a great deal of the content of courses is forgotten or half-remembered. Sometimes quite hazy notions survive alongside experiences of placements in schools where concerns they had were submerged because of the number of problems which so many children brought with them. Other difficulties arose when the ethos of a school in relation to child protection did not conform to the picture painted by those who had provided the training.

Once we have a planned approach to initial teacher training, guidance could then be issued to local authorities about their responsibilities in relation to newly qualified teachers and the provision of in-service sessions for all teachers. The other priority is, of course, in relation to the training of designated teachers who should be the source of experience, knowledge and support in relation to child protection in schools. In the first place local authorities must ensure that all newly appointed designated teachers do receive some training to enable them to meet their responsibilities. But the training dimension goes beyond this and must encompass ongoing training and support. Some local authorities already do this and have developed models that deserve to be replicated elsewhere. However, in many areas it is absent or so pedestrian as to fail to attract busy professionals. Sometimes teachers fail to attend multi-agency training at all or do not stay for the whole session. Feedback from the organisers reflects frustration with schools, whilst teachers point to the impossibility of being out of their establishments for more than one day. Although not exclusively the case, most of those attending multi-agency training from education are experienced designated or senior members of staff. Anecdotal comments are beginning to emerge questioning the value of attending if the subject matter is merely a reinforcement of what is known and practised and has been covered on other occasions. These are people who need to use the time available for training very thriftily and are beginning to demand a more sophisticated approach to its content and mode of presentation.

On the other hand, there are still many teachers who need basic child protection training and regular updating. Whilst it may be appropriate for this to be done by a designated teacher it would be advisable for it to be undertaken in co-operation with a child protection worker who would be able to bring a wider perspective. In this way the process of referral and subsequent decision making processes could be discussed and debated.

A clear approach to training would be very welcome, as would clarity about a school's contribution to case conferences. The issues differ quite considerably between primary and secondary schools and will depend, in part, on the effectiveness and shape of the school's pastoral system. In primary schools, if it is knowledge of the child that is required or monitoring the child's future safety, it should probably be the class teacher who attends a conference. In other circumstances it may be more appropriate for other members of staff to attend. In a secondary school the form teacher may or may not have had the chance to get to know the student, depending on how that system is organised. It may or may not be more appropriate for a year head or other colleague to attend. In both sectors the decision about whether or not the designated teacher goes alone, or is accompanied by a colleague, or does not, in fact, attend at all should be made on the basis of factors other than the financial necessity. The issue of when conferences are held may need to be examined and if a school is involved some consideration should be paid to the school's timetable. Teachers already have many meetings after school so even timings outside the school day may prove difficult, but the problems involved should not stop the imperative to try alternatives.

The response from schools sent a clear message that while they are willing partners in child protection teachers need support, and this is needed at a number of levels. At the most basic level they need support in dealing with parents and protection from possible parental reprisals. Although there are very few reports of this type of behaviour the number of attacks on teachers by parents is growing every year. So it is not surprising that there should be a level of apprehension. In this respect the situation is similar to that facing social workers. It may be a disproportionate response to think in terms of panic buttons or alarms but if this would reassure teachers it may be a necessary response. On the other hand as many schools have instigated rigorous vetting procedures at the entrance to schools it may be necessary to filter all visits through a specific door. It would seem entirely appropriate for a head teacher or senior member of staff to deal with parents when there had been suspicions of abuse, although many primary schools, in particular, are wedded to an open door approach which allows parents ready access to class teachers. Whatever the barriers it is clear that the issue has to be addressed.

Teachers wrote that they also wanted professional and personal support for themselves. This would obviously take different forms. The first line of support for a class teacher who has identified abuse or to whom a disclosure has been made is the designated teacher. It should be their responsibility to ensure that any immediate support and advice is available, although it is a much broader task to provide the ongoing support which may be needed. Some schools and some LEAs have established counselling services for their staff, while others have stress management programmes in place. Unfortunately these are very few and far between and most designated teachers are left as the main source of support, sometimes drawing on any other professional help that may be available to the school, such as the school nurse or a counsellor working with students. So this is hit and miss. But so is the support which may or may not be available to a designated teacher. Unless the LEA has made this a priority, and this is very unlikely, it probably will not be available at all. Teachers, unlike social workers, do not get regular, one-to-one supervision as a normal part of their job. There is no doubt that child protection work is potentially very stressful. At a time when it is recognised that the level of teacher stress has risen considerably it may be that some form of supervision should be considered as an investment in skilled and experienced staff.

But teachers were also concerned about the support they were allowed to give to their students around the time of a disclosure and subsequently. There are teachers who are afraid to say the wrong thing and jeopardise an inquiry. There are also those who are uncertain about what they can say at a later date. Some of the concerns could probably be allayed with appropriate training. Their responses went beyond this and focused on those students attempting to come to terms with the aftermath of abuse while being expected to follow a normal routine in school. Most respondents wanted them to have access to counselling in the school. Whilst school counsellors are more common than they were even five years ago many schools still do not have access to such a service and most of those who do have very limited access. Counselling and advice services for young people across the country fail to meet the level of demand or need. There was hope that the Government would make school counselling services a priority. However the emergence of the Connexions initiative indicates that the priority may be too focused on training and skills to address the wider spectrum of problems. Primary schools will not be touched by this initiative and are even less likely to have counsellors. It is time to recognise that most abuse will leave a wound unlikely to heal of its own accord. The healing process will vary enormously but as a society we have a responsibility to contribute to it. Many young people are left to get on with it on their own and teachers are often faced with the consequences of their behaviours as they work it through. Counselling in school, or accessed through school, can help to alleviate the feelings of loneliness and despair that often lead to antisocial or destructive behaviour.

The difficulties explored above will not all disappear of their own accord. The school's role in relation to child protection becomes more complicated as further layers of guidance and procedures are added. It is now well over a decade since the Government issued the first circular to schools dealing specifically with child protection and it has been a time when all agencies have been coming to terms with fresh and revised responsibilities in relation to children. The learning process is continuing with the new *Working Together* document (Department of Health et al., 1999) and the *Framework* document (Department of Health et al., 2000). It would be an appropriate time to take a fresh look at how schools are functioning within a multi-agency approach. Although Hallett's work (1995) was done before it would have been possible to measure the real effects on schools' response to the deployment of designated teachers in schools, the designated officer at Local Education Authority level and the increased training provision, it is probably true to say that while there are schools and Local Education Authorities that have achieved a very high level of professional practice, there are still many schools in need of significant further support to even begin to feel confident in this arena.

The challenge is how best to provide this support. The role and responsibilities of LEAs have been constantly brought into question in recent years. Some have been publicly condemned as a result of poor inspection reports and private organisations have been brought in to run their affairs. So far these have all been authorities with very high levels of social and economic need. The effect on the issues discussed here has yet to be assessed. It is now clear that the very future of LEAs is in doubt. If they survive they are likely to do so in a very different form. Schools' accountability to them will certainly diminish and yet the area of child protection is one that requires a degree of centralisation and co-ordination.

In Europe, initiatives such as Zones d'éducation prioritaires (ZEP) in France, Education Action Zones in England and the Education Priority Policy Programme in the Netherlands are examples of government policies which have targeted resources on disadvantaged areas. In time they will be evaluated which will enable the benefits of area-wide initiatives to be assessed. Even when the services exist they may be available in such a fragmented form that they offer too little, too late. It is possible that the extent of the problems facing schools across many countries will require a level of co-operation between agencies which legislation and policy makers have failed to reach. The problems presented by their pupils and students combined with the pressures on schools to raise educational achievement for all is driving some to forge alliances with other services and agencies. Even where services exist the ways in which they operate often fail to provide the level of support needed. It is clear that schools are not capable of, nor should they be responsible for, meeting the extent of the need with which they are presented. Teachers are now expected to take on many tasks for which they have not necessarily received training but which take up a considerable amount of their time. Access to help from other professionals will not only reduce the burden on teachers but should ensure a more developed and integrated response to the problems which arise.

In theory, education social workers or education welfare workers would support schools and pupils and in some areas this has been the case. They have played a crucial role in helping schools fulfil their responsibilities in relation to child protection, while providing help for individuals and families. However, for many post holders, the role has evolved into one where the main focus is on raising attendance in schools. Sometimes this has gone hand-in-hand with a more general welfare approach, but without a firm commitment this aspect of the work is being squeezed. And it is possible that this will become more apparent as LEAs devolve the money spent on this service to schools to spend as they see fit.

In a school-based approach to integrated services for children, services are provided to children and families through a collaboration between schools, the Health Service and Social Services. In general it is usually part of a larger movement to strengthen the economic, social and physical well-being of communities. Service integration and community development are often twin initiatives. The USA has been at the forefront in introducing projects to address this issue. More attention is rightly being focused on the social-emotional adaptation and educational progress of all children. There is a growing recognition that these two elements of a child's life cannot be separated and are mutually dependent. Many countries are looking for ways of achieving a better integration of services for school age children. For example, the 'School of the 21st Century', also known in some states as Family Resource Centers, was an idea that came out of the work of Zigler (Zigler, 1987). It is a school-based child-care and family-support programme that puts the school at the centre of co-ordinated community initiatives.

In the UK the Government is considering the establishment of 'one-stop' centres incorporating schools, health centres, and Social Services offices on some of the country's most deprived estates as part of the effort to address social exclusion. The proposal comes out of the work of the Government's Social Exclusion Unit and the proposed model is that of 'full service schools'. (See DfEE, 2000) The 'full service school' is a comprehensive approach to school-linked services combining school restructuring with service delivery:

The vision of a full service school puts the best of school reform together with all other services that children, youth and their families need, most of which can be located in a school building. The educational mandate places responsibility on the school system to re-organise and innovate. The charge to community agencies is to bring into the school health, cultural events, welfare, community policing and whatever else may fit into the picture. The result is a new kind of 'seamless' institution, a community oriented school with a joint governance structure that allows maximum responsiveness to the community, as well as accessibility and continuity for those most in need of services. (Dryfoos, 1994)

Full service schools exist in the USA and in Canada. Amongst the advantages identified are the opportunities for multi-agency teams of professionals to work together and to consider alternative approaches to problems, as well as providing strategies for earlier intervention. Pilot projects of full- or part-service school networks are currently being established in various parts of the UK.

Pilot projects on school sites incorporating health and social service provision have been introduced into Aberdeenshire. Their 'New Community School' approach was an extension of the integrated delivery of support services to children and families. The pilot phase has identified a number of issues which need to be addressed. These include :

■ the need for better integration of initial professional training for teachers, community workers, social workers and health professionals

■ the importance of team building and support in relation to joint working

■ difficulties facing professionals in delivering key national initiatives because of different funding streams and different management structures

■ operational difficulties caused by different professional codes of conduct and conditions of service and separate professional standards.

The Oldmeldrum Academy is due to open in August 2002 and the plan is to develop a model that could be followed by others. The outcome of all the pilots will provide valuable information on the conditions needed for effective multi-agency work.

The school's role in relation to child protection, and more generally child welfare, seems to be well established at a policy level but there are still many opportunities for it to unravel. This may be as a result of poor liaison with Social Services for a myriad of reasons, uncertainty as to roles and responsibilities or a failure to recognise when an issue needs to be taken further. In many authorities, education has failed to assume a profile within the multi-agency approach commensurate with its role in relation to children in its care. Perhaps this is due to some confusion of role that has never adequately been resolved. It may also stem from the expectation and constant pressure put on schools to achieve ever better results amidst claims that children's backgrounds should not be a barrier to their academic success. And, of course, this should be the case. But there is no doubt that children's backgrounds do have an effect on their readiness to learn and many schools are trying to cope with very damaged and desperate children. Schools are not able to meet all the needs of, or solve the problems of, those children who are at risk. At a time when schools are increasingly under pressure to raise the achievement of all children they are faced with problems which challenge society at every level. It is to be hoped that the initiatives such as Sure Start will help to alleviate such problems but for the immediate future it is time to take a fresh approach to the school's role in this area. For a range of reasons maybe Area Child Protection Committees have to adjust to a new direct responsibility for schools, rather than one mediated by the LEA. It would give substance to a truly multi-agency approach which could be reflected in one set of policies, procedures and guidelines across the area which would then inform a training programme. It may also force a really joined up approach on government departments and local authorities.

6 Recommendations

NSPCC is about to embark on research that will examine in detail the child protection process in schools in a number of LEAs and how these schools work within a multi-agency context. In the meantime, on the basis of the work reported in the previous chapters, it is appropriate to identify those areas needing further action.

■ OFSTED has a responsibility to inspect child protection policies and procedures in schools and LEAs to judge whether they conform to the guidance given by the DfEE. It is important that all teams have a consistent approach to the task and that they include discussions with representatives of the school community to ensure that they have a full understanding of the policies, procedures and their implementation.

■ Teachers have a vital place at case conferences and it is important for LEAs to support their presence in every way possible, including a funding formula which recognises that some schools need to attend a significant number of child protection conferences and associated meetings.

■ There is a clear need for schools and Social Services Departments to liaise over the timing of conferences and the information required from each.

■ All schools should receive guidance on their responsibilities to make sure that newly qualified teachers, newly appointed members of staff and students on placements with them are aware of their child protection policies and procedures.

■ Training for all teachers and other members of school communities in child protection should be an ongoing activity. Particular emphasis should be on the identification of the signs and symptoms of abuse as well as on how to deal with putting together various elements that may have aroused their suspicions.

■ All teachers should receive some training about case conferences and their role in these and associated meetings.

■ Support should be provided for teachers in:
    dealing with parents on matters of child protection
    supporting children and young people who report abuse
    supporting colleagues who deal with child protection issues.

■ There needs to be improved liaison between Social Services Departments and schools in the hope of improving each service's understanding of the other, combined with a more extensive use of multi-agency training for all teachers and social workers.

■ When Social Services Departments receive a referral, they should inform the school about the action taken or if no action is taken the reasons.

■ A regular reminder should be sent from LEAs to schools about schools' responsibilities in relation to child protection issues and the training opportunities that are available.

■ A helpline, or other form of support service, should be introduced in every area to give schools the opportunity to discuss concerns before they decide if it is appropriate to make a referral.

■ Further work is needed to identify the support that independent schools receive in dealing with child protection issues and the additional support that may be required.

■ Student teachers and newly qualified members of the profession should receive appropriate training to help them deal with any demands they will encounter in their early years in the classroom. This needs to be supported by high quality materials designed to ensure that all teachers have a solid understanding of the issues involved and which could subsequently be used as reference material.

References

Abrahams, N., Casey, K. and Daro, D. (1992). Teachers' knowledge, attitudes and beliefs about child abuse and its prevention. *Child Abuse and Neglect, 16,* 229-238.

Audit Commission. (1994). **Seen But Not Heard.** London: Audit Commission.

Baginsky, M., Crisma, M. and Melief, W. (2000). **Counselling and Support Services For Young people Aged 12 – 16 Who Have Experienced Sexual Abuse.** Report to the Daphne Initiative Office of the European Commission. (Summary available from NSPCC, London.)

Barker, R. W. (1996). Child protection, public service and the chimera of market force efficiency. *Children and Society, Vol. 10,* 28-39.

Birchall, E. (1992). **Report to the Department of Health: Working Together in Child Protection; Report of Phase Two: A Survey of the Experience and Perceptions of Six Key Professionals.** Stirling: University of Stirling.

Birchall, E. and Hallett, C. (1995). **Working Together in Child Protection.** London: HMSO.

Butler-Sloss, Right Honourable Lord E. (1988). **Report of the Inquiry into Child Abuse in Cleveland 1987.** London: HMSO.

Campbell, H. and Wigglesworth, A. (1993). Child protection in schools: a survey of the training needs of Fife schoolteachers. *Public Health, 107,* 413-419.

Corby, B. (1990). Making use of child protection statistics. *Children and Society, 4 (3),* 304-314.

Creighton, S. and Noyes, P. (1989). **Child Abuse Trends in England and Wales 1983-1987.** London: NSPCC.

Department for Education and Employment. (1995). **Protecting Children from Abuse: The Role of the Educational Service (Circular 10/95).** London: DfEE Publications.

Department for Education and Employment. (1998). **Teaching: High Status, High Standards (Circular 4/98).** London: DfEE.

Department for Education and Employment. (2000). **Schools Plus: Building Learning Communities.** London: Stationery Office.

Department of Education and Science. (1988). **Working Together for the Protection of Children from Abuse: Procedures within the Education Service (Circular 4/88).** London: DES.

Department of Health, Home Office and Department for Education and Employment. (1999). **Working Together to Safeguard Children: A guide to inter-agency working to safeguard and promote the welfare of children.** London: Stationery Office.

Department of Health, Department of Education and Employment and Home Office. (2000). **Framework for the Assessment of Children in Need and their Families.** London: Stationery Office.

Dryfoos, J. G. (1994). **A Revolution in Health and Social Services for Children, Youth and Families.** San Francisco: Jossey-Bass.

Elliot, I. (1996). **The Management of Child Protection Referrals within Schools.** Unpublished Thesis.

Gilligan, R. (1998). The importance of schools and teachers in child welfare. *Child and Family Social Work, 3,* 13-25.

Hallett, C. (1995). **Inter-Agency Co-ordination in Child Protection.** London: HMSO.

Harris, A. (1994). *Student learning experiences in pre- and post-reform courses.* In I. Reid, H. Constable and R. Griffiths (Eds) **Teacher Education Reforms: Current Research.** London: Paul Chapman.

Hinchcliffe, D. (1993). **Child Protection Under Threat.** London: Labour Party Publications.

Home Office, Department of Health, Department of Education and Science and Welsh Office. (1991). **Working Together Under the Children Act 1989: A Guide to Arrangements for Inter-Agency Co-operation for the Protection of Children from Abuse.** London: HMSO.

Jackson, S. (1994). Educating children in residential and foster care. *Oxford Review of Education, 20,* 267-279.

Jenks, C. (1996). **Childhood.** London: Routledge.

Kirkland, J. P., Field, B. and Hazel, A. (1996). Child protection: the continuing need for training and policies in schools. *Pastoral Care,* March 1996.

Maher, P. (1987). **Child Abuse: The Educational Perspective.** London: Basil Blackwell.

Michael Sieff Foundation Spring Conference, March 1994. **Working Together for Children's Welfare: Child Protection and the Role of the Education System.** Virginia Water: Michael Sieff Foundation.

Murphy, M. (1995). **Working Together in Child Protection.** Aldershot: Arena.

NSPCC. (1994). **Protecting Children – A Guide for Teachers on Child Abuse.** London: NSPCC.

Sinclair, R. (1998). **The Education of Children in Need.** London: National Children's Bureau.

Sinclair, R. and Jacobs, C. (1994). **Research in Personal Social Services: The Experience of Three Local Authorities. A Report to the Department of Health.** London: National Children's Bureau.

Tite, R. (1993). How teachers define and respond to child abuse: the distinction between theoretical and reportable cases. *Child Abuse and Neglect, 17,* 591-603.

Waldfogel, J. (1998). **The Future of Child Protection: How to Break the Cycle of Abuse and Neglect.** London: Harvard University Press.

Wattam, C. (1992). **Making a Case in Child Protection.** London: NSPCC.

Zellman, G. (1990). Linking schools and social services: the case of child abuse reporting. *Educational Evaluation and Policy Analysis, 12*(1), 41-55.

Zigler, E. (1987). **A Solution to the Nation's Child Care Crisis: The School of the Twenty-First Century.** Paper presented at the First Anniversary of the Bush Center for Child Development and Social Policy, New Haven, CT.

Inquiry Reports

Richard Fraser London Borough of Lambeth, Inner London Education Authority, Lambeth Southwark and Lewisham Area Health Authority (Teaching). Published May 1982.

Lucy Gates London Borough of Bexley and Greenwich and Bexley Health Authority. Published July 1982.

Jasmine Beckford London Borough of Brent and Brent Health Authority. Published December 1985.

Appendices

Appendix A

Letters and questionnaire sent to initial teacher training course in institutes of higher education and SCITTS

MB/stk/5.3.31

September 1997

Dear

Child Protection on Initial Teacher Training Courses

This research is the result of co-operation between the NSPCC and the University of Loughborough.

The questionnaire that is enclosed in this mailing has been designed to provide a clearer picture of what is included on Initial Teacher Training Courses in relation to Child Protection. All information will be treated in absolute confidence. No institution will be named at any stage in reports which result from the research .

A separate sheet is included for any individual who wishes to receive any additional information on this area, but this may be returned under a separate cover and to another named person if this is preferred.

We have enclosed three copies of the questionnaire. If there are more than three courses and additional copies of the questionnaire are needed or if you wish to clarify any point do please contact me.

It is hoped that the questionnaires will be returned by 1st October 1997.

I should like to thank you in anticipation that you will be prepared to take part in this important piece of work.

Yours sincerely

Mary Baginsky
Senior Research Officer
Child Protection Research

enc: 3 copies of questionnaire

MB/stk/5.3.31
September 1997

«Title» «FirstName» «LastName»
«Address1»
«Address2»
«City» «PostalCode»
Dear «Title» «LastName»

Child Protection on Initial Teacher Training Courses

This research is the result of co-operation between the NSPCC and the University of Loughborough.

The questionnaire that is enclosed in this mailing has been designed to provide a clearer picture of what is included on Initial Teacher Training Courses in relation to Child Protection. All information will be treated in absolute confidence. No institution will be named at any stage in reports which result from the research .

A separate sheet is included for any individual who wishes to receive any additional information on this area, but this may be returned under a separate cover and to another named person if this is preferred.

We are enclosing one copy of the questionnaire. If additional copies of the questionnaire are needed or if you wish to clarify any point do please contact me. It is hoped that the questionnaires will be returned by **1st October 1997**. A stamped addressed envelope is enclosed.

I should like to thank you in anticipation that you will be prepared to take part in this important piece of work.

Yours sincerely

Mary Baginsky
Senior Research Officer
Child Protection Research

enc: 1 copy of questionnaire

Questionnaire for initial teacher training course

The information collected on this sheet will be treated in the strictest confidence but it will allow any outstanding questionnaires to be followed up and a profile of respondents to be drawn up. No individual, institution or consortium will be named or otherwise identified

Title of the Course ....

Name of Institution ....

Length of Course..

Full time/Part time course *Please delete as applicable*

Status of the respondent ....
(in relation to the course)

For the purposes of this questionnaire, Child Protection is taken to mean:

"the recognition of the incidence and significance of child abuse, the identification of the signs and symptoms of suspected cases, and an awareness of appropriate procedures for dealing with them."

1. **Child Protection element:**

a) Does the course contain a specific Child Protection element ? Yes/No Please delete as appropriate

   If No please go to **Question 9 and 10**

   If Yes please continue **Questions 2–8**

---

2. **In which term and in which year is this taught?:** Please tick which boxes apply

	Autumn	Spring	Summer
PGCE	☐	☐	☐
Year 1	☐	☐	☐
Year 2	☐	☐	☐
Year 3	☐	☐	☐
Year 4	☐	☐	☐

Other ....

---

3. **Placement of Child Protection element:** Please indicate at what point the Child Protection element is taught: Please tick the appropriate box(es)

after the first and before the final school placement	☐
after the final school placement	☐

---

4. **Length of Child Protection element:** Please tick the appropriate box

Less than one hour	☐
One hour	☐
One to two hours	☐
Two to three hours	☐
Three to four hours	☐

Other – please specify ....

---

5. **Methods of delivering Child Protection element:** Please tick all those that apply from the following list

	Taught	Assessed
Lecture(s)	☐	☐
Workshops	☐	☐
Discussion groups	☐	☐
Seminars	☐	☐
Distance learning material	☐	☐
Other reading materials	☐	☐

Other (please specify):..

Would you please attach copies of reading lists and other materials used, if any.

6. **Is the Child Protection element:** Please tick all that apply

Compulsory? ☐

Optional? ☐

Incorporated into other sessions or elements?★ ☐

★Please give details if applicable ....

....

....

7. **Content of Child Protection element:** Please tick which of the following are covered
The Children Act

Information about the *incidence* of child ☐

protection cases in schools ☐

Information about the *incidence* of child ☐

protection cases in society ☐

Case studies ☐

How to detect children at risk ☐

Procedures for dealing with suspected abuse ☐

Agencies responsible for dealing with abuse ☐

Other issues (please specify)...

8. **Teaching on the Child Protection element is by:** Please tick as appropriate

Institution lecturer or tutor, non-specialist in Child Protection ☐

Institution lecturer or tutor, specialist in Child Protection ☐

School teacher / headteacher ☐

Visiting speaker★ ☐

★Please give details of background / specialism ....

....

....

Please go to Question 11

9. **If there is no Child Protection element on the course,**

a) what is/are the reason/s why this element is not included?

....

b) Would you wish to include a Child Protection element? **Yes/No** Please delete as applicable

10. **If you wanted to include such an element or needed further support, who might you approach ?**

1 ....

2 ....

11. (For all respondents): National requirements for all teacher training courses

All courses of initial teacher training are required to meet statutory criteria., in particular the **Framework for the Assessment of Quality and Standards in Initial Teacher Training** (Ofsted/TTA, 1996) and the new **National Curriculum for Teacher Training** (DFEE, 1997)

What effects, if any, do you think that these two new requirements will have on coverage of Child Protection issues on your course(es)? Please tick as appropriate

	1996 Framework	1997 National Curriculum
No effect at all	☐	☐
Likely to increase coverage of Child Protection issues	☐	☐
Likely to decrease coverage of Child Protection issues	☐	☐

Other (Please give details) ....

....

....

12. Do you have any other comments about coverage of Child Protection issues in initial teacher training?

....

....

....

....

....

....

Please continue on attached sheet, if necessary

Additional Information:

....

....

....

....

....

....

Thank you for completing this questionnaire. We assure you that this information will be treated in confidence and no individual or institution will be identified.

MB/stk/5.3.31
September 1997

MB/stk/5.3.31
September 1997

«Title» «FirstName» «LastName»
«Address1»
«Address2»
«City» «PostalCode»\
Dear «Title» «LastName»

Child Protection on Initial Teacher Training Courses

This research is the result of co-operation between the NSPCC, Community Education Development Centre in Coventry and the University of Loughborough.

The questionnaire that is enclosed in this mailing has been designed to provide a clearer picture of what is included on Initial Teacher Training Courses in relation to Child Protection. All information will be treated in absolute confidence. No institution will be named at any stage in reports which result from the research .

A separate sheet is included for any individual who wishes to receive any additional information on this area, but this may be returned under a separate cover and to another named person if this is preferred.

We are enclosing one copy of the questionnaire. If additional copies of the questionnaire are needed or if you wish to clarify any point do please contact me. It is hoped that the questionnaires will be returned by **1st October 1997.** A stamped addressed envelope is enclosed

I should like to thank you in anticipation that you will be prepared to take part in this important piece of work.

Yours sincerely

Mary Baginsky
Senior Research Officer
Child Protection Research

enc: 1 copy of questionnaire

Appendix B

Letter and questionnaire sent to schools

Dear Headteacher

At the end of 1994 NSPCC produced an updated version of the booklet **"Protecting Children: A Guide for Teachers on Child Abuse"**. A questionnaire was enclosed in the early distribution and a reply was received from your school. The questionnaire included questions on the actual booklet but also on Child Protection policies, practices and procedures in schools.

We would now like to update those responses which provided a great deal of useful information and I am enclosing a further questionnaire which I hope you or a member of your staff will be willing to complete. It has been designed to take as little time as possible to complete because it is important that we obtain as high a response rate as possible in order to inform future policy. However a sheet has been attached for any additional comments which you may wish to make.

All replies will be treated in absolute confidence and no school, LEA or other agency will be named or identified in any other way. I look forward to receiving your response by **Monday 8 December 1997** and should be pleased to answer any questions which you may have in the meantime

Yours sincerely

Mary Baginsky
Senior Research Officer
Child Protection Research

Child protection in schools

* Name of Person Completing the Questionnaire:...

Designation:...

....

Name and Address of School: ....

....

* If you would prefer to stay anonymous please do so, but it would be helpful to us if you would state your designation and complete the section below.

Please indicate which of the following apply to your school:

LMS

Primary

GMS

Secondary

Independent

All age

Special

Please return by 6 February 1998 to :

Mary Baginsky
Senior Research Officer
Child Protection Research Group
NSPCC National Centre
42 Curtain Road, London EC2A 3NH

1. **Does your school have a designated teacher with responsibility for Child Protection?**

    Yes/No

2. **If Yes please give details of this teacher's position in the school e.g. Head Teacher, Deputy Head Teacher**

    ....

3. **Does the school have:**

    a) a policy for responding to child protection issues?   **Yes/No**

    b) procedures for responding to cases of suspected child abuse?   **Yes/No**

4. **Has your school's Governing Body appointed a Governor with responsibility for Child Protection?**

    Yes/No

5. **Has your school been inspected by Ofsted?**

    Yes/No

    If Yes :
    a) please give date of the inspection:

    ....

    b) did the inspectors (please ring the appropriate reply) :

    – inspect the Child Protection policy?   **Yes/No/Don't Know/No Policy in existence at time of inspection**

    – comment on the Policy?   **Yes/No/Don't Know/No Policy in existence at time of inspection**

    – discuss the Policy with the Head Teacher?   **Yes/No/Don't Know/No Policy in existence at time of inspection**

    – discuss the Policy with the designated teacher with responsibility for child protection   **Yes/No/Don't Know/No Policy in existence at time of inspection**

    – discuss the Policy with other members of the teaching staff to assess their awareness of it?   **Yes/No/Don't Know/No Policy in existence at time of inspection**

    – discuss the Policy with members of the support staff to assess their awareness of it?   **Yes/No/Don't Know/No Policy in existence at time of inspection**

    – discuss the Policy with the Chair of the Governing Body?   **Yes/No/Don't Know/No Policy in existence at time of inspection**

    – discuss the Policy with the designated Governor with responsibility for child protection?   **Yes/No/Don't Know/No Policy in existence at time of inspection**

– discuss the Policy with anyone else? **Yes/No/Don't Know/No Policy in existence at time of inspection**

If **Yes** please give details

....

....

6. **When applicable is the school represented at Case Conferences? Yes/No**

If **Yes** who attends Case Conferences – Please ring the most appropriate answer

Head Teacher who is the designated person with responsibility for Child Protection
Always/On most occasions/Sometimes/Never

Head Teacher who is not the designated person with responsibility for Child Protection
Always/On most occasions/Sometimes/Never

Designated teacher with responsibility for Child Protection
Always/On most occasions/Sometimes/Never

Head of Year **Always/On most occasions/Sometimes/Never**

Form Tutor / Class Teacher **Always/On most occasions/Sometimes/Never**

Other (please specify) ....

7. **The following statements each appeared in the replies to the previous questionnaire. Please tick the following statements with which you agree or put a cross next to those with which you disagree :**

a) We are always able to provide a written report for the Case Conference ☐

b) It is difficult to know who should attend Case Conferences ☐

c) We often receive inadequate notice of Case Conferences ☐

d) We usually receive full information about the case which will be
   dealt with at the Conference ☐

e) It is difficult to face parents at Case Conferences ☐

f) We would welcome additional training on how schools could best support
   Case Conferences ☐

g) Finding funds to pay for supply cover for teachers attending ☐
   Case Conferences is difficult for this school

h) We are able to provide cover for teachers attending Case Conferences
   from within the School ☐

Please comment on Case Conferences if you wish to do so

....

....

....

8. **Please rate the following statements on a scale of 1 to 4 to reflect any concern which you may have about each area, with 1 indicating a great deal of concern, 2 indicating some concern, 3 a little concern and 4 indicating no concern.**

The ability of teachers to recognise the signs of abuse   1   2   3   4

If you are concerned do you have any suggestion for how this may be addressed ?
(Please tick any sources of support which may be applicable.)

By support from inside the school   ☐

By support from the LEA   ☐

By support from Social Services   ☐

By support from another agency e.g.

Any additional comments ....

The vulnerability of teachers who report abuse   1   2   3   4

If you are concerned do you have any suggestion for how this may be addressed?
(Please tick any sources of support which may be applicable.)

By support from inside the school   ☐

By support from the LEA   ☐

By support from Social Services   ☐

By support from another agency e.g. ....

Any additional comments ....

Uncertainties about contacting Social Services   1   2   3   4

If you are concerned do you have any suggestion for how this may be addressed?
(Please tick any sources of support which may be applicable.)

By support from inside the school   ☐

By support from the LEA   ☐

By support from Social Services   ☐

By support from another agency e.g. ....

Any additional comments ....

The possibility of some teachers attempting to handle a situation without passing on information   1   2   3   4

If you are concerned do you have any suggestion for how this may be addressed?
(Please tick any sources of support which may be applicable.)

By support from inside the school   ☐

By support from the LEA   ☐

By support from Social Services   ☐

By support from another agency e.g. ....

Any additional comments ....

Communications between the different agencies involved in a case 1 2 3 4

If you are concerned do you have any suggestion for how this may be addressed?
(Please tick any sources of support which may be applicable.)

By support from inside the school ☐
By support from the LEA ☐
By support from Social Services ☐

By support from another agency e.g. ....

Any additional comments ....

Support for teachers who deal with abuse 1 2 3 4

If you are concerned do you have any suggestion for how this may be addressed? ☐

By support from inside the school ☐
By support from the LEA ☐
By support from Social Services ☐

By support from another agency e.g. ....

Any additional comments ....

**Lack of training/experience of most staff in
the area of Child Protection** 1 2 3 4

If you are concerned do you have any suggestion for how this may be addressed?
(Please tick any sources of support which may be applicable.)

By support from inside the school ☐
By support from the LEA ☐
By support from Social Services ☐

By support from another agency e.g. ....

Any additional comments ....

The handling of accusations made by pupils against teacher 1 2 3 4

If you are concerned do you have any suggestion for how this may be addressed?
(Please tick any sources of support which may be applicable.)

By support from inside the school ☐
By support from the LEA ☐
By support from Social Services ☐

By support from another agency e.g. ....

Any additional comments ....

How best to support/deal with children who disclose abuse   1 2 3 4

If you are concerned do you have any suggestion for how this may be addressed?
(Please tick any sources of support which may be applicable.)

By support from inside the school   ☐

By support from the LEA   ☐

By support from Social Services   ☐

By support from another agency e.g. ....

Any additional comments ....

Support for children subsequent to disclosing abuse   1 2 3 4

If you are concerned do you have any suggestion for how this may be addressed?
(Please tick any sources of support which may be applicable.)

By support from inside the school   ☐

By support from the LEA   ☐

By support from Social Services   ☐

By support from another agency e.g. ....

Any additional comments ....

Relationships with parents involved in Child Protection cases   1 2 3 4

If you are concerned do you have any suggestion for how this may be addressed?
(Please tick any sources of support which may be applicable.)

By support from inside the school   ☐

By support from the LEA   ☐

By support from Social Services   ☐

By support from another agency e.g. ....

Any additional comments ....

Lack of time to get to know pupils amidst competing demands   1 2 3 4

If you are concerned do you have any suggestion for how this may be addressed?
(Please tick any sources of support which may be applicable.)

By support from inside the school   ☐

By support from the LEA   ☐

By support from Social Services   ☐

By support from another agency e.g. ....

Any additional comments ....

The time taken up in dealing with Child Protection issues   1 2 3 4

If you are concerned do you have any suggestion for how this may be addressed?
(Please tick any sources of support which may be applicable.)

By support from inside the school   ☐
By support from the LEA   ☐
By support from Social Services   ☐

By support from another agency e.g. ....

Any additional comments ....

If you have any other concerns not included above please provide details.

....

....

....

....

**9. Has the designated teacher with responsibility for Child Protection
     received any appropriate training?**   **Yes / No**

If Yes please give details

....

....

....

**10. Have any other members of your current staff received any training on
Child Protection issues?**   **Yes/No**

If Yes please give details including who provided the training

....

....

....

11. Have any governors received training on Child Protection issues ?
                                                                Yes/No

If Yes please give details including who provided the training

....

....

....

12. Has any Child Protection training been supported by GEST funding?

Yes / No

If Yes please give details

....

....

....

13. Are there any particular areas and/or posts which you think should be targeted for training in the area of Child Protection?

....

....

....

14. If you wished to discuss a possible referral with someone is there anyone to whom you are able to turn to for advice?   **Yes/No**

If Yes who is this? .

....

....

....

If No would you welcome the opportunity to have this type of support?   **Yes/No**

15. Would you like more help and information on Child Protection issues?

Yes / No

If Yes would you welcome it from (please tick all that apply) :

Your LEA   ☐
Your local Social Services   ☐
Your local Area Child Protection Committee   ☐
NSPCC   ☐
A Trade Union   ☐
Other (please specify) .

....

An additional sheet is attached for any comments which you wish to make.

Appendix C

Letter and questionnaire sent to LEAs

September 1997

Dear

LEAs and Child Protection

I am enclosing a questionnaire which seeks to collect information on the current position of LEAs in relation to the advice, guidance and support given to schools on Child Protection.

I do hope that you are prepared to co-operate with this research and I shall provide at least a summary of the findings for all respondents.

All information provided on the questionnaire will be treated in confidence and no individual or LEA will be named or identified in any other way.

It is hoped that the questionnaires will be returned by 10 October 1997.

If you wish to discuss any aspect of the questionnaire please do not hesitate to contact me.

My direct line in 0171 825 2588.

Yours sincerely

Mary Baginsky
Senior Research Officer
Child Protection Research

Questionnaire for leas on child protection and schools

Please answer all of the questions and either delete where appropriate or tick boxes
as required

**1. Does the LEA provide written guidance for schools on Child Protection
issues? Yes / No**

If Yes:

i) What form does this take?

....

....

ii) Does it follow the principles of the ACPC Guidelines? (please tick one box only)

Completely ☐

Generally ☐

Substantially departs from them ☐

If there are any issues in which the guidelines do depart please give details:

....

....

....

2. a) Is the LEA represented on the ACPC?   **Yes/No**

If Yes what is the job title of the Representative?

b) Are schools represented on ACPC groups?   **Yes/No**

If Yes please give details:

....

....

....

**3. Does the LEA consider that it has any responsibility for Child Protection
in relation to:**

(a) Grant Maintained schools?   **Yes/No**

(b) Independent schools?   **Yes/No**

Please comment or give details if you wish to do so

....

....

....

4. Does the LEA provide any of the following in relation to Child Protection for:

	a) Grant Maintained Schools?	b) Independent Schools?
Documentary Guidance & Information		
Training		
Referral Reporting Route		
Professional Advice		
Other		

5. Does the LEA check that schools have: (please tick relevant box)

(In question 5 N/A refers to the situation where there are no Grant Maintained/IndependentSchools within the LEAs catchment area.)

a) *Written policies on Child Protection?*

LEA Schools
☐ Yes
☐ No

Grant Maintained Schools
☐ Yes
☐ No
☐ N/A

Independent Schools
☐ Yes
☐ No
☐ N/A

b) *Procedures in relation to Child Protection?*

LEA Schools
☐ Yes
☐ No

Grant Maintained Schools
☐ Yes
☐ No
☐ N/A

Independent Schools
☐ Yes
☐ No
☐ N/A

c) *Designated teachers with responsibility for Child Protection?*

LEA Schools
☐ Yes
☐ No

Grant Maintained Schools
☐ Yes
☐ No
☐ N/A

Independent Schools
☐ Yes
☐ No
☐ N/A

d) *Procedures to communicate the policy/procedure to all staff?*

LEA Schools
☐ Yes
☐ No

Grant Maintained Schools
☐ Yes
☐ No
☐ N/A

Independent Schools
☐ Yes
☐ No
☐ N/A

e) *A nominated Governor with responsibility for Child Protection?*

LEA Schools
☐ Yes
☐ No

Grant Maintained Schools
☐ Yes
☐ No
☐ N/A

Independent Schools
☐ Yes
☐ No
☐ N/A

---

6. **Does the LEA offer your own schools a consultation service on Child Protection?**

Yes/No

If Yes please specify for which types of school:

If **Yes** is this through Education Welfare Service/ Other? (please specify):

....

....

If **Yes** is this included in relevant documentation distributed to schools?   **Yes/No**

7. **Is Child Protection training included in the LEA's Training programme for schools?**

Yes/No

If **No** is there a reason(s) for this?

....

....

8. **Does the LEA provide training in child protection issues for the following people? (Please give details of the levels of training provided and the organisations from which the trainers are drawn.)**

Designated teachers **Yes/No**

....

....

Pastoral Staff **Yes/No**

All teaching staff in schools **Yes/No**

....

....

All teaching / non-teaching staff (Whole school training) **Yes/No**

....

....

Peripatetic staff ....**Yes/No**

....

....

Governors **Yes/No**

....

....

Others – Please specify for whom:

....

....

9. **Please give details of the proportion of schools which have been represented on Child Protection training during the past three years:**

LEA primary schools..

....

GMS primary schools...

....

Independent primary / preparatory schools...

LEA special schools...

....

GMS special schools..

....

Independent special schools...

....

LEA secondary schools...

....

GMS secondary schools ....

....

Independent secondary schools ....

Other eg Pupil Referral Units ....

Please comment if you wish to do so

....

....

....

....